CW00348131

Disclaimer

This book is not intended as a substitute for the medical advice of physicians. The reader should regularly consult a physician in matters relating to his or her health and particularly with respect to any symptoms which may require diagnosis or medical attention.

Ann Bowditch does not assume and hereby disclaims any liability to any party for any loss, damage or disruption caused by errors or omissions, whether such errors or omissions result from negligence, accident or any other cause by using any of the disclaimers within this book.

Introduction

1. About Ann

When her practice was opened in 2012, Ann quickly made a name for herself on the island of Guernsey. She has had tremendous success in helping people overcome anxiety and many other issues. Ann has put her knowledge and experience with clients to good use in this book.

Ann is passionate about her work and keen to help people feel more empowered. It is well reported that people who take responsibility for, and part in, their own healing process will make better progress than those who do not.

Ann's work encompasses a wide range of therapies. She has a way of communicating with people that helps them to see new perspectives and can often be life-changing. Ann is a passionate therapist who is prepared to speak truthfully and is recognised for her commitment to her work and clients.

Ann Bowditch GQHP, GHR Reg., META-P

Dip (Hyp) Hypnotherapy
EFT (EFT International Certified)
Matrix Reimprinting Practitioner
Meta-Health Practitioner
Colour Mirrors Practitioner & Teacher
RMTi Consultant, NES Health Practitioner
MBIR Practitioner

2. Anxiety and Energy

Just about every action and every thing has energy. A thought has energy, as does the spoken word. You have no doubt experienced when you meet up with someone who is happy and positive, how this boosts your mood. You then experience the opposite feeling when you meet someone who is very negative and draining; you can feel as if they have sucked the life out of you. Although both situations contain energy, they carry very different energy vibrations.

Anxiety has energy too. Because energy is flexible it can be transformed into something much more positive.

To break free of anxiety, trauma must be resolved within the subconscious mind. Relaxation and other techniques can help too. It is helpful to understand what sets off anxiety and work through those triggers. Learning and setting new perspectives can also be crucial to well-being.

Many anxiety sufferers lack self-esteem and self-confidence and a high proportion suffer with depression. Other people may experience emotions such as anger, impatience, intolerance and become introverted or appear fussy. Anxiety can show itself in many different ways.

This book is a result of my experience in helping hundreds of people overcome anxiety. This is not your average 'break free of anxiety' book. It is the result of tackling many aspects of anxiety, many of which are not spoken about. However your anxiety manifests itself, it is not something that you have to live with.

3. How to use this Book

This book is effectively split into three sections:

1) About Anxiety
2) Foundation for Change
3) Exercises

By absorbing the information in this book and carrying out the exercises, you will have the chance to make wonderful changes to your life and lift the cloud of anxiety. Please take your time, absorb the information, practice the exercises and create a plan for your good mental health.

Do not look upon this book in the same way you would a novel. The ending is important but no more important than the start and the middle. Read and re-read, make notes, discuss, allow thoughtful reflection, ask yourself questions like: "How does this apply to me?"

I have also included mantras. You can use the ones in this book or create your own. Mantras help re-programme the mind and your energy system. Even if at first you don't believe in them, try them and give them time to work.

Always use mantras in a positive sense so that they focus on what you **do** want. Print out mantras and place them in key places such as in your purse or wallet, on your desk at work, in your bedroom, in the kitchen, wherever you will see them on a regular basis. You may like to add them to your phone too.

Please also visit www.energyofanxiety.com to view additional information and support.

SECTION 1
ABOUT ANXIETY

A bit of background to help you
understand why you are anxious.

4. What is Anxiety?

*"Anxiety is taking away the now
and living in fear of a future which is unlikely to happen."*

Ann Bowditch

Anxiety is a term used to describe a combination of symptoms related to feelings of fear or nervousness. Along with the physical symptoms common in anxiety such as shortness of breath, tension, dizziness, dry mouth, clammy hands, clouded thinking, nausea, racing heart; many people who suffer anxiety worry a lot and have many negative thoughts. They tend to focus on the worst-case scenarios, which in turn aggravates the anxiety. Long-term anxiety can affect sleep, health and general well-being.

Anxiety comes in many different forms but there are two basic types. The first is Generalised Anxiety or Generalised Anxiety Disorder with the other type being Specific Anxiety.

Generalised Anxiety Disorder

Generalised anxiety disorder (GAD) is the term given to a condition whereby the sufferer experiences chronic worry and tension thus causing high levels of stress. This term was introduced in 1980 when anxiety neurosis was split into GAD and panic disorder. GAD became a diagnostic classification in the third edition of the *Diagnostic and Statistical Manual of Mental Disorders.* Sufferers think of the worst-case scenarios, run these over and over in their minds and expect them to happen.

GAD can be all-consuming and stop people doing basic tasks such as going to the shops or holding down a job. GAD can be incredibly debilitating for some people and impact on every aspect of their lives. Other people can function, apparently, normally with GAD, whereas in fact many people wouldn't know they had this anxiety.

Often GAD is experienced in individuals where:

- there is no specific event which triggered the anxiety in the first place.
- they may have had a parent/guardian who worried a lot or was depressed.
- they may have suffered birth trauma or other trauma at a very young age.
- they feel they have 'always' worried or suffered with anxiety.

Specific Anxiety

I consider someone to have specific anxiety if one of more of the following criteria are met:

- A specific event, or group of events, has triggered the anxiety.
- The person has not always suffered with anxiety.
- The person's anxiety is triggered only in specific situations.

Does it matter which anxiety you have in terms of treatment?

It helps me, as a therapist, to understand the specific nature of a person's anxiety, even if their anxiety is of a more generalised type.

When someone suffers with GAD, there is a benefit in working with the subconscious mind to resolve any trauma and create positivity. However, teaching sufferers techniques is also hugely important. I usually find those with GAD need more treatment than people with a more specific anxiety. It is also likely that they will always need to take care of their mental and emotional health, in the same way that someone with gastrointestinal issues has to take care of their digestive system on a long term or permanent basis.

For anyone who has anxiety triggered by a specific event, it is hugely beneficial to seek out and resolve the memory of that event held within the subconscious. It is also helpful to learn techniques that can be instantly called upon at any time.

5. The Anxiety Brain

"The brain is amazing. It can be our worst enemy or our best friend depending on how we use it."

Ann Bowditch

The Anxiety Brain is a term I use to refer to that over-analysing behaviour and natural protective mechanism.

The role of the brain in anxiety is broken down into key structures within the limbic system, which is directly involved with memory, behavioural and emotional responses. It is not imperative for you to remember these components and what they do in order to break free from the patterns of anxiety.

The Limbic System

The limbic system structures are situated above a layer of the brain called the brainstem. The brainstem is responsible for vital functions including respiration, digestion and reproduction. It is critical for issues of survival and forms part of the old brain, known as the reptilian brain.

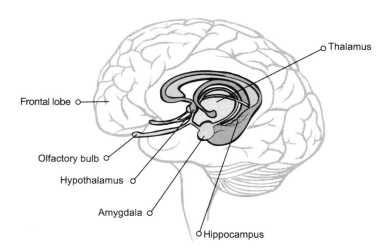

The following are structures within the Limbic System linked to anxiety:

- Thalamus
- Hypothalamus
- Hippocampus
- Amygdala

The Thalamus

The thalamus comprises two prominent bulb-shaped masses. Its main function is that of a sensory relay station. It processes sensory information and relays this information to another layer of the brain called the cerebral cortex.

The things you see, hear, taste and touch come through your nerves and end up in the thalamus. These senses can serve as memories to events and are linked to emotions. This does not include the sense of smell, because smell bypasses the thalamus and has its own private sensory system.

Think about some music which makes you feel really energised or really good in some way and play it or just sing along to it in your head. One of my favourite songs is *'The Only Way Is Up'* by Yazz & The Plastic Population. When I hear it I feel good. I recall memories from 1988 and listening to that song in a nightclub. I can remember who I was with and what life was like then. Both good and bad events turn into memories stored within the mind and we make strong associations to certain events through our senses.

The Hypothalamus

Although very small, the hypothalamus is linked to many systems in the body. The hypothalamus controls the endocrine system, which regulates the release of hormones into the blood stream. It regulates the autonomic nervous system, which is broken down into two different parts; namely the sympathetic nervous system and the parasympathetic nervous system.

Sympathetic Nervous System – When we are anxious or stressed, the hypothalamus stimulates the endocrine system to release stress hormones. The most commonly known are adrenalin and cortisol, which are linked to the fight or flight response, which I cover in more detail later on.

Parasympathetic Nervous System – this is referred to as 'rest and digest'. This is the calming part of the system. When we are mostly functioning in this system, we are able to relax and revitalise both mind and body, creating good health both mentally and physically.

The Hippocampus

The hippocampus is named after the Latin for seahorse due to its shape. It is the part of the limbic system, which directs many bodily functions. There is one hippocampus located in both the left and right hemispheres of the brain.

The hippocampus is the part of the brain which encrypts threatening events into memories. It then connects emotions and senses to these memories. This is so we can recognise these memories again and link them to similar scenarios. We can then, in an instant, recognise the current situation as pleasant, stressful or threatening, based on our catalogue of stored memories. It effectively converts short-term memories into long-term memories.

The Amygdala

The amygdala is an almond-shaped set of neurons located deep in the brain's medial temporal lobe. It plays a key role in the processing of emotions and is linked to both fear responses and pleasure. You can look upon it as a communication hub between the parts of the brain that process incoming sensory signals and the parts that interpret those signals.

Information comes into the amygdala, which processes the information and decides how to respond. In terms of anxiety this would, again, be the fight or flight response.

The amygdala can be linked to many emotions and responses when stimulated, such as anger, violence, fear and anxiety.

Importantly the amygdala makes associations with events, which form future responses to events. If those events are interpreted as bad, scary, nasty or any other negative emotion, this may cause future problems when faced with similar events.

The emotional memories stored in the central part of the amygdala may play a role in anxiety disorders involving fears, such as fear of dogs, spiders or flying.

The Process in a Nutshell

Information Comes into the Brain

That Information is Processed by the Brain

Information is Interpreted as Safe/Unsafe (this may be based on previous events/information already stored)

⇓

Depending on whether the interpretation is considered Positive or Negative, or Safe or Unsafe, the Stress Response, also known as the Fight or Flight response, may be triggered.

The Subconscious

In theory the subconscious is looking out for us. If you have a traumatic memory, for example you were bitten by a dog when you were three years old; at twelve years old you will most likely not consciously remember the event but your subconscious has the event stored away.

Imagine you are then invited to a friend's house and these friends have a dog. When you see the dog, suddenly you feel anxious, even panicky. You aren't sure why but your subconscious knows why. It recalls the event from when you were just three years old, flags this new dog situation as 'similar' and puts you on your guard – it advises that *"you are in danger!"*. *"You either need to run the hell out of here or you need to be ready to confront the problem."*

This happens very quickly, if not instantaneously, followed by anxiety symptoms such as clammy hands, shortness of breath, heart beating fast, feeling fearful, clouded thinking, etc. This occurs so quickly you do not have an opportunity to consciously process the situation and recognise you are, in fact, safe.

In order to prepare your body to run or fight, the chemistry of your body needs to rapidly change, to make you as fast and powerful as possible.

Those stress hormones come into play, pumping around your body creating those physical changes you recognise as anxiety. You do not have a choice in this because your subconscious is far quicker than your conscious mind to react. In reality your subconscious is looking out for you. This is part of your natural survival mechanism.

The most common symptoms of the fight or flight response are:

- shallow breathing, which may lead to hyperventilation
- heart racing
- clammy hands
- perspiring
- clouded thinking
- digestion shuts down
- more blood and oxygen goes to working muscles
- shaking
- limited blood flow to extremities results in a feeling of cold or tingling
- dilated pupils
- nausea

The stress response is an amazing piece of body chemistry and is there to help us. It dates back to our ancestry, when we needed to fight off a tiger or run from it in an instant.

In this modern age, we do not need to fight tigers and we rarely need the fight or flight response to be so easily activated. However, if you are about to be attacked by a crazy person with a knife then you will be very grateful for the fight or flight response.

What does all this mean?

The anxiety you experience has a root cause. It is not an accident or freak of nature. It has a starting point and by addressing the root causes, we can calm things down. It is not always initiated by a trauma, although in many cases it will be trauma which has triggered the anxiety.

How do we take more control of that limbic system?

I have found a combination of methods to be successful in addressing anxiety, namely:

- Breathing Techniques.
- Bring some yin (calm energy) into your life.
- Create a balanced exercise routine.
- Set up positive 'triggers'.
- Practice positive visualisation.
- Gain new perspectives.
- Establish a positive mind-set.

We are now going to cover these areas over the course of the book.

6. The Curse of Fear

"The fears we don't face become our limits."

Robin Sharma

We naturally have only two fears: the fear of falling and the fear of loud noises. So how did all these other fears such as fear of flying, spiders, snakes, dogs, speaking in public, clowns, heights, germs, death and the hundreds of other fears, come about?

Fear is linked to our base chakra. Chakras are energy vortexes throughout the body. The base chakra is about our need to survive. Back to our ancestry this would have been related to needing shelter, food and protecting ourselves as well as our family. Later in this book, we'll discuss chakras in more depth.

In the world we live in now, we operate under those principles at the basic level of need for survival. However, our fears largely relate to modern day issues such as having sufficient money week to week or for our retirement, being liked by others and public speaking. If we worry too much about potential problems, we will activate our fear response also known as the fight or flight response which may lead to a panic attack.

The first sign of snow and the shops sell out of the basics because we go back into our ancestral fear pattern of the worry of there not being enough provisions, even though many of us have chest freezers and kitchen cupboards stocked up with enough food for the next three months.

Our basic needs are the same as they were centuries ago but we have modernised them for the era we are living in. Taking it to another level, some people now activate their fear response if they lose their mobile phone, have to put their point across, attend a social gathering or a host of other possibilities.

"Do not allow fear of what may happen later today, tomorrow or next week take away today's happiness."

I am going to break down how we become fearful in so many, non-threatening, situations.

Learned Fears

I recall, as a child, a fairly large sized spider running up my mum's arm when she was sweeping the floor and her moving back quickly trying to flick the spider off her, looking rather frightened and making panicky noises. This most likely triggered a fear of spiders for me. The body of the spider was probably about the size of a thumbnail. So compared to the size of us, it was actually tiny. How many house spiders actually attack us or threaten our lives? Most likely none, yet so many people have spider phobias.

Some of the areas of life responsible for spreading the fear are:

- News stories
- Television and films
- Social media and the internet
- Friends and family – talking of their experiences
- Negative thinking
- Newspapers and magazines
- People over-dramatising events

I have clients come to see me to eliminate their fear of flying or other fears and they are worried that their children will pick up on their fear subconsciously and then have the very same fear. This is possible, as they would have 'learned' the fearful behaviour.

As small children, especially before the age of six years old, we are absorbing information at an incredible rate. If you saw your Mum or Dad jump at a incy wincy spider, it was a message to your subconscious that spiders are dangerous and to be feared. However, if your Mum or Dad had picked up the spider and said how cute it was and placed it outside, you would have looked on them in a much more trusting and less fearful way.

Life Events

Let's take a look at how you might create a fear of flying. Let's assume Jim does not have a fear of flying. He goes on a flight to Spain and the plane hits turbulence all of a sudden. The plane is bumping around, plastic glasses and trays are flying about all over the place. There are no announcements from the cockpit and the cabin crew rush to their seats. There is a woman a few seats ahead who is screaming, a baby crying and Jim starts to feel queasy.

Jim's thoughts start to become negative; I don't like this! What the hell is happening? Why hasn't the pilot said anything? We are going to die! Jim's subconscious soaks all of this information up. It notices the fear in Jim and those around him. It recognises what appears to be an urgent and potentially dangerous situation and says *"get the hell out of here!"*

Jim's heart rate starts to rise, his palms get clammy, he cannot think straight, his body generates more adrenalin, which is a natural stress hormone, to deal with the situation and his breathing becomes shorter and quicker. In a worse case scenario, he struggles to breathe and has a panic attack.

Within just a few minutes everything calms down, the pilot comes over the public-address system and apologises for the disruption. He calmly tells the passengers they had hit a bit of turbulence. Jim now knows there was no danger, yet his subconscious isn't going to start back pedalling now and pretend none of that happened. It has already created a belief of "flying is dangerous" or "flying is unsafe". To overcome this Jim will most likely benefit from some help to clear the trauma, such as hypnotherapy, unless he is able to tap through his own fear!

Jim carries on normal life and puts the event to the back of his mind. Months later his partner suggests booking a holiday and he thinks "what a fabulous idea". So they decide to book a holiday to Morocco. About a month before Jim is due to fly, every time he thinks about the flight he starts to get hot and sweaty. Jim cannot help but have negative thoughts; "The flight is going to go down." "I'm going to die".

That amazing subconscious of Jim's, which is always trying to do its best for him, is sending him a strong message; *"what the hell are you doing going on a plane again, don't you remember last time you went on a plane you nearly died?"* **Of course he didn't nearly die, the plane hit a bit of turbulence. He was in fact perfectly safe.** However, his subconscious retained the fear from the memory of that event, and the fact he actually landed safely appears irrelevant and ignored. When the subconscious has formed a belief, it is rare you are able to rationalise with it using just conscious thought or will power. More needs to be done to change the belief by working with the energy system and/or subconscious mind.

It is possible Jim is not aware of any specific thoughts about flying but feels anxious at the thought of flying because **the subconscious reacts much quicker than the conscious mind.**

If Jim doesn't get the fear addressed, his subconscious mind starts to recognise other events as potentially 'dangerous'. This is because his subconscious has recognised that when he was on the plane he was in an enclosed environment. So when he is in another enclosed environment such as a lift or in small rooms, he goes into the fight or flight mode. And this results in another fear. The fear of flying has escalated to a fear of small, enclosed spaces.

There is good news though. Very often resolving the original root cause event within the subconscious can bring all the fears tumbling down like a stack of dominoes.

Escalation of Fears

Traumatic event on Plane – Perceived as Dangerous

⇩

Fear of Flying

⇩

Subconscious also interprets enclosed spaces as dangerous

(because inside a plane is an enclosed space)

⇩

Fear of Enclosed Spaces

Primitive Reflexes

There is another reason people can be fearful or anxious and this is due to some of the primitive reflexes not being integrated or becoming activated. Primitive reflexes are related to the first part of the brain to develop and should only remain active for the first few months of life.

When reflexes are not integrated they are referred to as being 'retained'. There can be a number of reasons for retention of primitive reflexes. Issues such as the mother being ill or suffering stress during her pregnancy, a traumatic birth experience such as forceps or caesarean section may also lead to retained reflexes. Other reasons for retained reflexes may include: trauma, lack of floor play as a baby or toddler, illness, head trauma and vertebral subluxations.

A vertebral subluxation is a response to stress. When stress hits, the muscles go into spasm and the spinal bones effectively lock up. This causes the nerves travelling through the spine to be irritated or even choked. This affects nerve communications between the brain and body, resulting in a loss of control and regulation of the body. This may lead to various health issues from a bad back to gastrointestinal issues.

Another issue may arise that could impact reflexes after they have been integrated and this may cause certain reflexes to become active. This can happen at any time in life and is usually due to stress, trauma or illness.

So, let's take the earlier turbulent flight experience which could have activated your Fear Paralysis Reflex. Therapy can resolve the issue as the Fear Paralysis Reflex no longer has a need to be active in that type of situation.

However, if you are someone who appears to be generally fearful in life and worry a lot or have become that way and have found therapy to be unsuccessful, I suggest you seek out someone trained in dealing with primitive and postural reflexes such as a consultant of Rhythmic Movement Training International (RMTi). They can help you integrate your reflexes.

Fight, Flight or Freeze

All three of these responses relate to stress and trauma and are triggered by our natural inbuilt security system. This is because the subconscious mind is aware of a perceived harmful event or believes there is some sort of threat to your survival. As we have learnt earlier the fight or flight response is quite simply an automatic reaction to fight or run away based on a primaeval reflex that would have been related to a real life-threatening situation.

We have the third response, which is the freeze response. It has become apparent over recent years that by not releasing the freeze response this causes us to hold onto trauma. The freeze response is another part of our physical structure and also links back to our ancestry. When the tiger had cornered us and was about to devour us, our brain had assessed the situation and decided there was only one option remaining, which was the freeze response. When you activate your freeze response you have run out of all other options. There is no opportunity to run or fight, you feel helpless and hopeless. You are in serious danger. "I cannot run or fight, I must therefore freeze or die."

It's highly unlikely we will get attacked by a wild animal in this modern day unless we put ourselves in dangers way, yet this natural instinct to freeze is still ingrained in us. We therefore apply the freeze response to situations which are stressful. Some of which may be serious or dangerous.

Usually the freeze response happens in more seriously traumatic events such as being threatened with a weapon, being involved in an accident or being sexually abused or raped. However, it can happen in what appear to be less serious events, if at the time you have no option to flee the situation or fight, such as a teacher telling you off as a child or being bullied. The brain decides there is only one option remaining, which is to go into the freeze response. You are most likely unaware of the freeze as consciousness appears to shut down.

In the freeze response you go into a self-paralysis protection mode. You become physically, mentally and emotionally immobilised, which results in you consciously being unable to feel or experience the distressing event. Perhaps you can recall an event when you felt you could not move or speak. It is only after the event you consider how you could have dealt with it.

In the freeze response you effectively hold the trauma because humans do not automatically discharge the freeze response. This can result in psychological, emotional and physical challenges following the harrowing incident. Very often this is referred to as Post Traumatic Stress Disorder or PTSD.

Wild animals discharge the freeze response as soon as possible after the incident. If you wish to see this, I suggest you conduct an internet search for "animal release of freeze response". It is quite an amazing natural process to view. I must warn you prior to watching, it is not the most pleasant thing to view but once the freeze response has been released the animal has let go of the trauma and can go about its business. If we did the same, we would not have so many fears. This is one example of how amazing the mind and body are when nature takes its true course.

Because we are so domesticated, we do not usually discharge the freeze response and therefore stay stuck in the trauma. This means we develop fears and phobias and may struggle to deal with certain situations.

These traumas need to be released in order to free you. I would only ever recommend dealing with such situations under the guidance of a suitably qualified therapist. Someone who works with the subconscious mind such as a hypnotherapist or a practitioner of Emotional Freedom Technique or Matrix Reimprinting. Of course, if you feel any other appropriate therapy works well for you then go with it.

Should you wish to work with me – my details can be found towards the back of the book.

Fear has Energy

Just like every other emotion, fear carries an energy vibration, a very low vibration. When you are in fear you struggle to think clearly and will rarely find solutions. **Most things you fear will not happen.** Please remember this fact.

The energy you give out is the energy you get back therefore you will just keep attracting more things to be fearful of. Your mind will get into the pattern of negative thinking and always expecting the worst.

Remember what I said, **most things you fear will not happen!** Fear is often based on the past with a focus towards the future, but in reality we only have now. When you step into the now, you realise you are okay. The past has already happened and is behind you. You cannot control it. The future is yet to come and so you cannot control that either. So, in effect, you only really have now to consider. Anxiety is often the result of trying to control situations and then realising you cannot control everything. **Take a breath and recognise right here, right now, you are fine.**

When I fall into fear, and I do, even knowing everything I know about the mind fear creeps up on me sometimes, I recognise it as just energy. I tell myself *"it's just energy"*. Fear is not a tangible object, you cannot pick it up, you cannot touch it and you cannot see it. At the point you fall into fear remind yourself *"it's just energy"* and you created it. That's right, you created it! Therefore it is within your power to liberate yourself from it. Tell yourself *"it's just energy, it's not tangible, it's not real and it's not happening"*. Energy can transform and change very quickly. Tell yourself *"right here, right now, I'm ok"*. As you do this more often, you will be able to let go of unnecessary fear very quickly.

If you have trauma, no matter how apparently irrelevant or minor, seek help to resolve it. What is absorbed as trauma to one person may be completely insignificant to another. No matter what your trauma is, it is important and relevant to you. Do not regard it as insignificant. Do not refer to yourself as silly or stupid because you have fears and beliefs. They are there for a reason but can be overcome. If you were bullied, were in a car crash or were abused, get your trauma resolved, especially if it is impacting your life.

Just a final note on fear and the three responses of fight, flight and freeze. These are mechanisms that ensure our safety when activated in a response to a life-threatening event. However, when they become active due to events such as stress, family arguments and worries then we need to develop new perspectives and learn techniques to deal with them.

This book is going to help you achieve this. Your fight, flight and freeze responses will still be there for you when needed but let us work on developing new skills and a new mind-set for life that means you activate them much less often.

EXERCISE– Don't Skip It!

Take my five-step approach for disposing of fear in the moment:

1. Recognise fear as just energy; it's not a tangible object.
2. You created it therefore you have the power to be free of it.
3. Remind yourself – right here, right now – you are okay, even if you are in the middle of an episode of turbulence. You are here and alive enough to feel the fear, therefore you are okay.
4. Notice where in your body you feel the fear. If it is in your stomach for example, give it a colour. Imagine the colour is spinning in one direction, stop it and now imagine it spinning in the other direction and have it change colour. Keep focusing on this until it dissipates. The feeling was just energy and, as I've said, energy can change.
5. Change your focus onto something else. Recall a time when you felt good and recall the positive feeling or pick up an object and focus on it for at least a minute.

If the fear comes back, repeat this process. Each time you do you will be diluting the fear. If you do not feed the fear, it will diminish. **Fear only remains active if you are giving it the attention and energy to stay.** Don't put your attention into something you don't want in your life.

7. Beliefs and Brain Waves

*"If I accept you as you are, I will make you worse;
however, if I treat you as though you are what you are
capable of becoming, I help you become that."*

Johann Wolfgang von Goethe

When we are very young and naïve we believe just about everything we are told. We believe in Santa Claus, the Tooth Fairy and many other fairy tales. Infancy is a wonderful time; we are so innocent and trusting at this time in our lives. This has a lot to do with the different types of brainwaves we possess.

Delta Brainwave Frequency

In the womb babies are in the Delta brainwave frequency, nice and relaxed. We continue in this frequency until the age of around two years old. As adults in the Delta frequency, we are usually unconscious, in a deep dreamless sleep, with very little, or no, critical analysis happening. This state is associated with production of serotonin, the happy chemical.

Theta Brainwave Frequency

From age two until the age of six years old our brain waves are mostly in the Theta range, also referred to as the 'state of hypnosis'. This is why young children daydream and do not analyse situations. In this phase we are very open to suggestion, absorbing the world and everything around us, accepting what we are told as true. This is a super powerful learning state. In this state, children are effectively little sponges, absorbing information about the world around them.

As adults in this Theta frequency we feel wonderfully relaxed, even dreamlike. This is a state of deeper hypnosis or meditation; a state of inspiration and insight, which is perfect for problem solving. We can find answers in this state which, when we are in a more stressful condition, are just not available to us.

Alpha Brainwave Frequency

A change or cross-over begins around the age of five years old towards the Alpha brainwave frequency, when the analytical mind takes shape. Children become more consciously aware and start to ask questions. They may not be automatically satisfied with the answer they are given, as they are more critically aware now. This is a good state for learning and is still quite a relaxed and stress-free state.

For adults, Alpha is a pleasant state and is common when undergoing meditation and hypnosis. We feel peaceful and calm in the Alpha state. Here, creativity is flowing and easily accessible. Fears and phobias can melt away in this state. The Alpha frequency acts as a wonderful bridge between the conscious mind and the subconscious mind, which is why it works so well for hypnotherapy.

Until around eight years old children may be switching between Theta and Alpha depending on the stage of their personal development.

During this period, whatever happens in our lives is critical to our belief system and the way we address and see the world. Our belief system contains information linked to what we think about ourselves, what we think about other people and our beliefs about the world at large too.

The Belief System

I recall one client who came to me suffering with anxiety and very low self-esteem. She would refer to herself as *"stupid"*. She clearly was not stupid. I only needed a minute in her company to realise that.

I took her back to a memory from when she was just four years old. She was at school, but outside and walking down a slope. She hadn't realised that in order to keep her balance, she needed to lean back a little. She lost balance and fell over, the teacher said to her *"you are stupid"*.

This one comment stuck with her, it sunk into her subconscious mind, she was in the Theta brainwave frequency at just four years old. She absorbed the comment and believed it without question and there began a 40 year belief of *"I am stupid"*. We did some work around this memory and she began to have a lot more belief in herself.

I am sure the teacher had no idea of the long term impact such a comment would make. While in those specific brainwave frequencies, if we have nothing to compare with, we will absorb what we are told without question and that becomes our belief. What then happens is every time you make a mistake or say or do something which isn't correct, it confirms the belief *"I am stupid"*.

Imagine a set of scales. On one side your scales say *"I am clever"* and on the other *"I am stupid"*. The first stone went on *"I am stupid"*. The first belief is very important because it gives the subconscious its first point of reference. It is as if the belief has ten times the power of the other possible belief *"I am clever"*. Every new mistake is another stone added to the *"I am stupid"* side.

Now she is eight years old and someone tells her she has done something really well, which should mean a stone can be placed on the *"I am clever"* side. However the mind kicks in and says, hold on, that does not compute because I strongly believe *"I am stupid"*. Just look at my scales, they clearly show *"I am stupid"*. This stops the stone going on the *"I am clever"* side to bring the scales more into balance.

When has someone paid you a compliment or told you you've done something really well and you haven't allowed yourself to take it in? This could be an insight into your beliefs about yourself.

What things have been said to you which have caused you to form beliefs during your youth that may have set your scales of self-belief in a negative way? Chances are you will not recall all of these comments or events consciously.

Here are some possibilities:

Comment	Belief
"His brother is the bright one"	I am thick/stupid
"Monkey face"	I'm ugly
"Well, try harder"	I'm not good enough
"We like Jason better"	I'm not popular

What events have happened to you which have caused you to form beliefs, about yourself, others and the world at large?

Here are some examples:

Event	Belief
Failing an exam	I'm stupid
Watching the news and seeing wars and other traumatic events	The world is a dangerous place
Being on a flight when there is some nasty turbulence and people are panicking	Flying is dangerous
You get bullied	I'm all alone in the world/I am powerless
Your mum panics when she sees a dog off its lead running towards her	Dogs are scary/dangerous
You give a wrong answer and everyone laughs at you	It's not safe to speak up

We do not necessarily form all our beliefs by the time we are six years old. Therefore events, which happen to us after this age, can still influence our belief system.

Our belief system sets our internal programming for how we deal with life and is therefore key in forming our habits and behaviour.

Here are some examples:

Belief	Habit/Behaviour
I'm stupid	Do not try/avoid exams or putting self forward
The world is a dangerous place	Want to stay safe at home and not travel or go to big events
Flying is dangerous	Avoid flying or needs medication to fly
I'm all alone in the world/I am powerless	Feel insecure and anxious
Dogs are scary/dangerous	Scared of dogs – goes into fight or flight when see a dog
It's not safe to speak up	Never speak up, hates socialising

Consider some of the habits and behaviours you would like to change and what beliefs may be linked to those.

When we experience shock or trauma, we know we are activating certain areas of the brain (refer to Chapter 5). In the state of shock, when we are in the fight, flight or freeze response, we transition from the conscious to unconscious state. At this point, the traumatic event becomes a memory, which enters and is stored within the subconscious mind. This event and our interpretation of it may cause us to form a new subconscious belief. This can happen at any stage in our life.

However, we can effectively reverse this process using the same, Theta brainwave state, which is why hypnotherapy can be hugely beneficial. By inducing the state of trance, this gives us access to the huge memory, databank or library of information we have stored, often outside of our conscious mind. We can then make the changes necessary to allow for a more beneficial belief system.

The Theta state is a powerful frequency from which to initiate change. The good news is that a therapist will rarely need to go through every awful event in someone's life to create the positive behavioural change needed. Very often a professional need only address the most significant events or a few key events. This has a 'domino effect' as other related negative scenarios weaken, causing the negative belief and resulting behaviour to be overridden by a more positive belief and behaviour.

For example, someone who has been bullied throughout their life may not need to resolve every subconscious memory they have of bullying. It may take resolution of just one or two memories to make the desired change. The subconscious is so powerful when we use it in the most positive way. I've seen so many amazing changes in people.

Change can be more powerful and sometimes simpler than you could ever imagine. I recall one client who came to me for weight loss. You may be aware that weight problems are often associated with emotions and traumatic events.

My client accessed a memory from her youth when she was sexually abused. We addressed the memory. We then completed the course of treatment.

The last I saw of her she had lost seven stone and was in a very happy relationship and pregnant. I have no doubt she had subconsciously gained weight in order to protect herself from further abuse, either to create more physical protection (layers) or to make herself less attractive to future possible abusers. The work was done in a trance state and it beneficially changed her life.

A therapist can work with these Alpha and Theta brainwave frequencies using visualisation, positive affirmations and other techniques to create change. It is not all about going into the memory though. The techniques in this book will also help you.

Below are the other brainwave states.

Beta Brainwave Frequency

The Beta brainwave frequency is our normal awake and alert state of being – our conscious state. This is the state of critical analysis and logic. It is the 'thinking' state of mind. In the Beta state the *inner voice* is apparent. We may worry and be fearful. Our more negative moods will be accessible in this state. Anxiety and depression are more active in this state too.

Gamma Brainwave Frequency

The Gamma frequency was discovered more recently. Gamma is reported to have the fastest frequency. Research suggests Gamma brainwaves are associated with high-levels of information-processing and cognitive functioning.

The Gamma state is said to be one of peak mental and physical performance, accessed when 'in the zone'. It is the state of transformation. People with very high levels of Gamma activity are said to be highly intelligent, compassionate, with impressive memory recall and strong self-control. It is the state of higher learning and focus.

Summary

We are able to transform our emotions and feelings about previous life events to create a more positive belief system. A positive belief system will help us to create more beneficial habits and behaviours. Spending more time in the Theta and Alpha frequencies will put us in a state more open to these positive changes and move us away from the anxious and fearful states.

It is beneficial to spend some time in Theta and Alpha brain frequencies by introducing relaxation techniques or undertaking tasks which keep your mind occupied in a more hypnotic way. Meditation is a very good way of achieving this state.

I would like to make a point about meditation. People say to me *"I can't meditate"*. However, that belief just depends on what you think meditation is. Meditation for many of us is just like anything else, we may not be very good at it the first time we try but if we practice we can get better at it. If you drive, do you remember how many times you drove before you felt you were a competent driver? If you have played a sport, learned an instrument or done any number of things, were you brilliant on your first attempt?

Occasionally in life you come across a natural, someone who is brilliant first time but I bet even Roger Federer wasn't ready to win Wimbledon the first time he picked up a tennis racket. So my message here is **be compassionate with yourself and give yourself time to practice.**

When you first meditate, you may be completely in your conscious head with thoughts all over the place, about what you are having for tea, what the weather is doing and generally making a list of jobs you need to do. But the more you practice the better you will get. You may never get to the point where you have no conscious thoughts, people rarely do, but you will benefit from practice. There are other ways to get into these beneficial brain states, as noted below.

Action

Spend time in Alpha and Theta brainwave frequencies every day. In an ideal world I would suggest you spend an hour on this but anything is better than doing nothing. So, if you can only find ten minutes, then give your best effort and attention in the time you have allocated. Set an intention to gain the greatest benefit from your chosen activity.

Here are some suggestions to help you get there:-

- Meditate
- Listen to relaxing music or play an instrument
- Practice craftwork and creativity such as colouring or painting
- Close your eyes and visualise
- Watch a sunrise or sunset
- Take deep breathes
- Try some light exercise like Tai Chi
- Have a Reiki or any other treatment
- Watch the sea, moon or stars
- Walk on the beach or countryside

By spending more time in these frequencies you are giving yourself a break from anxiety and re-training your brain. This opens you up to more positivity and finding beneficial solutions.

You can also use these frequencies to implant positivity. Just before you go to sleep you are in a suggestible state. As you feel yourself dropping off to sleep, plant some positive suggestions such as *"I am a calm and relaxed person"*, *"I feel better each day"*, *"I am resourceful and can deal with any situation"*, or create a suggestion of your own.

SECTION 2

FOUNDATION FOR CHANGE

How you look at life, and life's experiences, is critical to what you believe, how you act and whether you create the life you want.

8. Owning Anxiety - Stop It!

*"Anxiety does not empty tomorrow of its sorrows,
but only empties today of its strength."*

Charles Spurgeon

If you have never seen the Bob Newhart sketch entitled "Stop It" have a look for it on the internet. If only most of our problems could be solved this way, life would be easier but I would probably be out of a job.

However, there is a serious point to this. When people are ill for a long period of time, whether that is physically, mentally or emotionally, they tend to refer to their health issue as "my arthritis", "my diabetes" or "my anxiety". Talking in this way suggests an attachment.

You need to stop this! It's not a pet "my dog", it's not your house, it's not something you want to own, you didn't go out and look for it, you didn't buy it, you didn't ask for it. Stop owning it. While it becomes 'yours', there may be a reluctance from your subconscious to let it go. Or when it is gone, your subconscious may try and find it again. So when you refer to anxiety, refer to it as "the anxiety" or "this anxiety" – it's not 'yours', it is something you have been experiencing, so stop speaking about it as if it is your possession.

If you are reluctant to let go of anxiety as your possession then there may be reasons behind this.

In short, that anxiety is not yours, you don't want it and you certainly don't want to own it. Therefore stop talking about it as if it belongs to you. STOP IT!!

9. Change is Good

"Progress is impossible without change, and those who cannot change their minds cannot change anything."

George Bernard Shaw

As you embark on this journey of self-development you will experience challenges. Challenges are what help us to learn about ourselves and life. They are to be embraced. One of those challenges may be the fact that others do not respond well to the 'new and empowered you'. They may say to you "you've changed". Well "hello" that is the idea! And do you know what? It's their problem if they don't like the fact you have changed. You can't hold back your progress for their sake.

As long as you feel you are a good person and act with integrity and good intent then, if someone has a problem with something you have said or done, it really is their issue, not yours. Some people close to you may feel threatened by the new you because it felt safe for them to keep you small. This is perhaps not a conscious thought on their part and nor is it necessarily deliberate or nasty towards you.

As you develop new levels of awareness or views, change some behaviours and generally become more empowered, they may feel threatened or confused because you are not small or boxed in any more. It may take them time to adjust and get used to it.

As you progress on your journey, you will lose some people along the way. You may feel they do not fit in with your life now or they may not want to be part of this wonderful new you. The old adage of friends for a reason, friends for a season and friends for a lifetime could not be truer.

You will begin to recognise the energy suckers; the people who suck the life out of you. I use a simple thought process when I am going to meet up with someone. I ask myself how do I feel about meeting that person? Do I feel energised? Do I feel exhausted at the thought, or am I excited or relaxed? How do you feel during the get-together and how do you feel afterwards?

If people energise you or you feel relaxed after being in their company or they have some other positive influence on you then it's good to have them in your life. It's important to recognise that you have choices in life and some people are just not for you. Be okay with that.

Many people believe they must do certain things and they are responsible for making others happy, when it is just not the case. Do you feel that you have been avoiding your natural feelings so as not to hurt others? When you truly pay attention to yourself you set yourself free. **Doing what is right for you is self-preservation not selfishness.**

When your actions are in conflict with your truth, you risk creating unhelpful behaviours, such as overeating, drinking, self-harming, gambling and other destructive habits. Not being true to yourself can cause depression and anxiety. Do you want to follow your truth or create 'dis-ease' within your mind and body?

As you continue on this wonderful exploration of life, you will start to connect with different people. You will connect with people who educate and guide you, people who are changing with you and people you aspire to be like.

Be open to change. Change is what enables you to grow and prosper, to find inner peace and live a happier and more positive life. When you start to act in the way that serves you best you feel empowered, you begin to love life so much more and lose those restrictions. Life falls into place because you create your life with the energy you give out to the world.

Allow yourself to be the truest form of yourself you can possibly be. Never let anyone else's judgement get in the way and certainly do not let others put guilt on your shoulders. You are better than that and deserve better than that. This is hugely important so I'm writing it in bold.

**Never let anyone else's judgement stop you being amazing.
Never let anyone else put guilt on your shoulders.**

Keep moving forward, sending out to the Universe exactly what you want to get back. Create the energy that says "this is who I am – fabulous me".

**If you want to be respected, respect yourself.
If you want to be loved, love yourself.
If you want to feel empowered, empower yourself.**

**Be honest with yourself.
Be the truest form of yourself you can possibly be.**

**Love your quirks.
Appreciate your qualities.
Know what you stand for.
Own your life!**

LOVE IT – BE IT – OWN IT!!

10. Confronting Negativity

"Negativity distracts me from my goals.
So I simply don't entertain it.
I'll also occasionally laugh at it as well."

Mama Zara

Your perspective is **your** reality.

I choose to see beyond negativity in order to find something positive. When I cannot comprehend events that have happened, such as hurting or killing people, I send love because the world always needs more love than it does hate or anger, not because I approve of what happened. I simply ask: "What if I bring love into this situation?" This question connects you with love and the energy will instantly change.

Negativity from others is *their* negativity. It is a reflection of them, their life, their beliefs, the way they have been treated and their attitude. A true, loving person would not be negative about you or towards you. A kind, caring, happy person would not pass on their negativity. Negativity from others is about them, not about you.

If someone is negative about the way you look, the way you behave, what you do or the job you hold, let them wade through their swamp of negativity like a crocodile, as you glide through the ocean of love and light, like a beautiful loving and playful dolphin, being amazing you.

If you do not fully accept yourself then
how can others accept you?

If you do not believe in yourself then
how can others believe in you?

If you want your life to change then it must start with you!

What we receive is a reflection of what we send out into the Universe. If you want acceptance, love, respect and belief then it starts right inside of you, in your gut and in your heart. You can wait for others to say you are amazing and some may do that but, until you feel it for yourself, it will never be enough.

When people are anxious they have a misconception, an untruth, about themselves because they often don't believe they have the capacity to deal with situations.

The truth is:

Whatever life throws at you, you will deal with it.

You are far more capable than you ever thought you were.

You are far more resilient than you ever thought you were.

You haven't yet accessed all the skills available to you and this is why you are anxious. You must now begin to stand in your power, feel the strength from your solar plexus, just below your ribcage, and start to believe in yourself. It is time to stand up to the world and say: **"This is me, I am here and very capable".**

11. Importance of Exercise

"Exercise has greater value than just pushing your physical limits, it is an essential part of physical, emotional and mental well-being."

Ann Bowditch

During exercise, neurotransmitters known as endorphins are released, causing a positive change in the brain chemistry. Endorphins are reported to be structurally similar to morphine and can therefore provide pain relief as well as feelings of well-being. This is why, following exercise, many people report that they experience a more positive mood. Regular exercise is also reported to create a greater feeling of self-control and help raise self-esteem.

Aim to make your exercise routines balanced. By all means, go and do a run, have a gym session or do boxing training, but also do less intense exercise which may require some calmer mental focus and body control.

The following examples can be very beneficial from a well-being perspective, many of which will work your core and give you good focus and body control:

- Tai Chi
- Yoga (there are many types so find something to suit you)
- Pilates
- Body Balance
- Swimming (especially good in open sea)
- Walking
- Stability ball exercises
- Bosu ball exercises
- Forms of dance
- Martial arts

I encourage you to do activities you enjoy and connect with. If you hate the gym then don't go to the gym. If exercise has never been your thing then explore the many possibilities as it can be fun. The benefits of exercise can be a gift for everyone.

12. Technology and Social Media

"Internet living is imaginary living. You cannot dip your foot in the sea, laugh with your friends, see the stars sparkle, or feel the rain on your face if you're living online. Live in the real world."

Ann Bowditch

You cannot write a book about self-development in 2019 and not include social media.

As I have been writing this, I have been constantly distracted by certain social media platforms mainly due to my love for animals. My personal page is almost totally consumed with cute animals, lost animals or animals who need a home. It is no wonder my newsfeed, mostly animal related, is a reflection of the information I share.

When I search online for a product such as a bicycle wheel, I am then flooded with adverts for bicycle wheels. This is a great metaphor that reveals that we get back what we give out. The same goes for positive or negative energy.

What energy are you putting out on your newsfeed? Are you playing the victim? In which case you are keeping yourself in victim mode. Are you looking for sympathy for your illness or injury? In which case you are more likely to keep yourself sick or injured for longer because it serves you a purpose.   Are you being angry? Are you feeding negativity into others' newsfeeds? If so, you are feeding the negativity and therefore keeping negative energy in your life.

Are you moaning about someone?   What benefit is putting that thread up except to create more bad feeling and keep you in negative energy? You create your own reality.   Don't feed the negativity – because it is like a fungus which spreads far and wide.

Many stories on social media may cause you to feel depressed or anxious. In fact, much of what you read on social media is untrue and yet people share it. Be aware of what you are choosing to bring into your consciousness.

Is your social media taking control of your life? Will you go out without your mobile phone or does the prospect of leaving your phone behind put you into a cold sweat? Most people are so emotionally attached to their mobiles they won't leave the house without them but, not so many years ago, we didn't have mobiles and we survived. Most people do not need to contact you urgently 99.99% of the time. Occasionally you may have something happening in your life where it's beneficial to have your phone but, be honest, do you really need it with you 24/ 7?

Give yourself some freedom, take a walk without your mobile. Have an evening free of your mobile and social media. Give your body a break from those cell phone electromagnetic fields.

I see people walking with their dogs, at bus stops, even cycling or driving, all focused on their mobile phones. It makes me wonder what they are missing out on.

Take a moment to think about how much of what you read on social media is useful or true. Some of it may well be helpful. It is a case of putting it in perspective and balancing your time because too much time on social media is taking away an opportunity from doing more productive, positive, mood-enhancing activities and putting your mind at peace.

We are putting so much pressure on each other to act instantaneously. We are losing any sense of balance in life. What changes could you make so you are less reliant on your mobile phone and make your use of social media positive but not too time consuming?

Sometimes we need to set our own rules for our well-being and good health such as to turn your mobile off two hours before bedtime and do not turn it on again until you have been up and about for a good hour. If this is a real problem for you then at least turn off those notification sounds.

I never allow mobile phones in the bedroom. If your phone is also your alarm clock, I suggest you get an actual alarm clock. I also turn WiFi off at night.

There are options now for limiting use of Apps. Put your phone on silent and away at meal times and when watching your favourite TV shows or when you meet up with a friend.

13. Changing Patterns in Your Life

"When you change your energy, the energy from others must also change because the dynamics have changed."

Ann Bowditch

What are the patterns in your life that you want to be rid of? Perhaps you notice patterns of abusive relationships or unfulfilling relationships, bullying, not holding down a job or lack of financial abundance. What happens in your life that causes you to say "this always happens to me?"

Not all patterns are bad. You may always win when you enter a prize draw, always be the last one to get through the green light just before it turns to red or always get home just before it rains.

I see patterns in my clients very much like the ones I have mentioned above, especially in relationships and bullying. One client came to me with a severe lack of confidence and suffering anxiety, she was bullied through seven years of school life. She had been in verbally abusive relationships and had a history of being treated badly. In work she held a top position but, despite others' belief in her, she severely lacked confidence in herself.

We started to work with her subconscious to liberate her from some traumatic events. We also worked on the energy she was giving off. In her case this was an energy of "I'm not worthy" or "you can walk all over me". We cleared the negativity of the past, as well as focusing on a brighter, more confident future. As she progressed through the treatment her energy changed and she started to step into her power.

This is what she said:

"After years of bullying throughout childhood and teenage years my self-esteem was extremely low and I lacked confidence. I was extremely insecure, had no self-belief and found it hard to believe that anyone would think any good of me.

After reaching an all-time low last year I decided it was time to seek help which is when I turned to Ann. She made me feel completely at ease from the start. I am now at a stage I honestly thought I'd never reach because I had become just the person I thought I was. But I have learnt that you can in fact retrain your mind and the energy you give off is truly what you receive back.

Ann has completely changed my way of thinking and I can't thank her enough for the help and support she has given me. Without wanting for this to sound like a cliché it has literally been life-changing for me, allowing me to live a much calmer and happier life. I no longer spend each and every day worrying about anything and everything and my anxiety has reduced significantly."

This goes to show when you commit to change and embrace the process, there is an opportunity to create a better life for yourself. You are what you give out. You create your reality. As this client says **"the energy you give off is truly what you receive back."**

Unhelpful and negative patterns are an energy that we are able to break out of or change. If you don't like the way things are, you can change things. We always have options.

Someone who constantly falls into abusive relationships is sending out an energy which opens them up to these relationships. They are not stepping into their power. This will link in with their belief system which needs to be addressed. They may have beliefs such as "I am not good enough", "I don't deserve to be happy" and "I always get things wrong". Their friends, partner or colleagues will prove this to be right by continuously abusing them.

These beliefs may not be something you are consciously aware of but held deep within the subconscious.

EXERCISE – Don't Skip It!

What is the pattern in your life that you would like to be rid off? Write it down.

Now write down anything that comes to mind about that issue? Spend at least ten minutes doing this. Once you do this, thoughts will start to flow through. Do not ignore anything you feel is irrelevant or incorrect. These thoughts may be vitally important to this pattern.

If there is someone who knows you well and that you feel comfortable talking to about this issue ask them to discuss it with you. Get their thoughts on how you relate to this as it may bring another angle into your understanding.

Focus on what you want to create now. Be open to possibilities. What is the new pattern you want to create such as self-confidence, to be more positive, or to have a fulfilling career?

It is important when you want to change things that you focus on what you DO want. I have clients come to me who want to lose weight. They have tried everything else; sometimes actual bariatric surgery. They may have been trying to lose weight for thirty years or even more.

I see the fear on their faces because they worry if this doesn't work they are doomed, never to be slim again. These people focus on being fat, they don't focus on being slim hence they are driving their subconscious and energies to focus on being fat. I tell them they must focus on what they want, ie to be slim. What will life be like when you are slim? What will you look like, how will you behave, what are the benefits of that behaviour?

The same goes for you. **You must open up your thoughts to what you do want.** If you want to be socially confident, imagine yourself going into an event with confidence, how will you stand, what will you look like, how will you converse with people? Focus on what you DO want.

Spend time imagining what your life will be like when you have what you want. Use as many senses as possible to imagine this – what you will see, hear, feel, smell and taste.

Write down how you will be acting differently and what your life will be like with this new positive pattern in your life.

Create an affirmation that fits this. Write down this affirmation and put it where you can see it every day and frequently during the day.

Repeat this affirmation, out loud when you can but also silently. Don't just say it…. say it like you **believe it!** Most importantly make it positive and say it like you have it already.

It must be in the positive. Not negative, such as *"I don't want to live in fear"*. Transfer that to **"I am courageous and calm".** Notice how these two slightly different phrases make you feel. The first makes you feel small and keeps you in the anxious mind, whereas the second is more empowering and has much more positive energy. Say it like you already have it. Own it. Never put limitations on yourself.

Here are some examples.

"My partner loves and respects me".

"I have all I need in the world."

"People respect and believe in me".

"I create opportunities in my life"

The more good work you do with your subconscious and with energy work around any issues the more you will achieve what you are seeking in life. It does work. I've seen this happen successfully so many times but you have got to do it for yourself. Sometimes you may need help and guidance but don't shirk this responsibility, embrace it, take responsibility for your life, your happiness and your future.

Create a picture board of things you want to bring into your life and how you want your life to be. Align your energies towards what you want. Believe it can happen. Even if right now you don't think it, pretend you do, then it will become a belief.

Include some personal goals on your picture board; *"I am going to run 5km by 21 October"* or *"I am going to go for a promotion in six months' time"*. This is all part of the energy changing process.

Channel your energy into what you do want. You have the ability to make the energy positive by your actions and internal processing. Every positive action you take is bringing more positivity into your life. Keep at it.

14. You are Not Your Past

"The past is my story, now is my glory, the future is my satori."

Ann Bowditch

Far too often we allow events of the past to dictate our present and our future. We allow the past to limit us in many aspects. It may limit our fun, achievements, expectations, potential and of course enjoyment of life.

It is true that events from our past are held within our subconscious. If I were being more precise I would go further and say those events are held within the cells of our bodies and within our matrix – so not just inside of us but outside of us too. That may not sound like the greatest news but if the anxiety you have suffered is due to events in your past then the great news is you can take charge of your life.

When I step into fear, I tell myself *"right here, right now I'm ok"*. Fear is usually about the future, often based on past events – fear is rarely about being in the 'now'. In 99.9% of cases, in the 'now' when you check in with yourself, you will realise you are okay. Do it now, check in with yourself, reading or listening to this book. How are you doing? You're okay right? I mean you are breathing, you are safe and you are not being threatened in any way.

We all have these negative thoughts, expectations of disaster but right now none of that is happening to you. It is time to cut your ties with the events of the past and live in the now. By all means take the learnings from those events. Understand they were gifts and lessons, even if you don't understand exactly what these are yet. New perspectives will help you understand these events. Resolve the past by releasing the emotional charge and changing the subconscious perception. Check in with now, and chill about the future.

I know most things I've worried about have never happened or if they have happened, they've not been in anyway as serious, problematic or disastrous as I expected or imagined them to be.

You are not your past but your behaviour and response to events is a by-product of your past. Your past has contributed to your beliefs about yourself, others and the world you live in. Your past has impacted on your self-esteem, self-confidence, behaviours and thoughts.

When events happened, those unpleasant events we therapists call traumas, you went into the fight, flight or freeze response. At that time you did not have access to the knowledge, skills and all the resources which were available to you because your system went into survival mode. This meant you were unable to assess the situation fully, most likely unable to speak up, possibly even unable to move. You could say a part of you shut down to protect yourself.

However, in a calm, relaxed state of mind you can access those memories and arm your 'younger self' with all you needed at the time. You have the wisdom of your older self, your higher self and the Universe in that calm state. You can bring in new and higher perspectives. You can take the learnings from the events and squash the negative beliefs you formed at the time whether those beliefs were about yourself "I'm not good enough", other people "people cannot be trusted" or the world "the world is a dangerous place".

If you were bullied as a child, you are not that child now.

If you were abused as a child, you are not that child now.

If you were made fun of as a child, you are not that child now.

You may need to heal that child and bring balance to your subconscious and energy system. Remember this: you are an amazing, wonderful, intelligent, resourceful, powerful and brilliant human being. This is a fact.

You may have created an energy about these past events which draws you into having continually been bullied, abused or made fun of but it's just energy, energy can be changed. Now it's time to step out of the negative energy and away from those negative beliefs to create the life you are worthy of and truly desire to have.

The limitations you feel are the limitations you put upon yourself based upon the past but you are not your past. You now have an opportunity to see yourself in a new light and create a more positive future.

You are not the sum of your mistakes. Most mistakes made are just a part of your life experiences, part of your learning and were created to springboard you into something better. Your mistakes do not define you, what does define you is your ability to continue moving forward towards what you do want.

I see this so often from my clients. As we resolve their traumas and discuss the issues I am referring to in this book. I see and feel their entire energy change, their demeanour changes, the way they behave and interact all change, for the better. I see the burdens lifting off their shoulders, I witness them feeling more positive about themselves and what they can achieve. I believe that deep down you already know all of this but when someone else tells you, it gives you permission to take action.

You could easily be one of those people who walks into my studio seeking change, which is why I know, when you allow yourself to move away from old patterns that are not serving you, you will change too in any way you want to.

Make a decision right now to acknowledge the past. Allow yourself to live in the now and create a bright future. When you worry or have a negative thought, consider that it may be related to the past. It is certainly related to past thinking and beliefs that you are moving away from. Acknowledge it, repeat one of the mantras below or create your own, and breathe into the now.

EXERCISE – Don't Skip It!

What do you believe about yourself? Write down a few beliefs. These beliefs will be based on your past, either relating something said to you or some event in your past.

Example:

I'm not good enough.
I must be perfect in order to be loved.
I am hopeless.

Create a plan to break free from these beliefs and create more positive beliefs.

<u>Example:</u>

I am going to write down everything I have done that is good, positive and successful.

From now on, I am going to gracefully accept compliments.

I am going to start by loving myself, physically and emotionally and recognise that I am splendid as I am. Each day I will select a part of my body and tell that part I love it.

I'm going to set myself a goal and work towards that goal. Something achievable but that requires commitment.

MANTRA

Repeat these mantras.

"I release myself from the past and live in the now."

"My mistakes are part of my life experiences but do not define me. My ability to make positive changes defines me."

15. Bullying

*"If people throw stones at you,
pick them up and build something."*

Anonymous

Many people who suffer anxiety have some memories of bullying. That bullying may come from any number and type of people such as a parent, sibling, school friends, colleagues, social acquaintances, teachers, religious figures, sports club and peers.

Once someone has been bullied, it can leave them feeling powerless and lacking self-esteem and confidence. It can also leave them in fear of ever speaking up. When you are bullied, especially in your childhood, this will most likely have caused you to form certain beliefs. These beliefs may be along the lines of:

- "I can't make friends"
- "I'm not popular"
- "I'm not good enough"

By resolving the trauma of bullying, it is possible to rebalance your beliefs and bring new perspectives to the situation, resulting in more confidence and higher self esteem.

Many people who are bullied fall into victimhood. It is hugely important to get out of the feeling of being a victim. When you are in victimhood, you are powerless and trapped in the negative energy.

To be and feel the way you want to be and feel, you must step back into your power and recognise you were bullied because the bullies seized an opportunity. Those bullies were really the powerless ones. They needed to feel big and strong and powerful so they sought out someone who could make them feel that way. They didn't pick on someone they thought may stand up to them, instead they picked on someone they thought they could abuse. How big and powerful is that? Of course it is weak and sad. Be curious about their behaviour, what caused them to be that way. It is sad for them – very sad.

If you want to change how an event impacts you, you have to let go of the emotion around it and find new perspectives. It is far easier to change yourself and your energy than to do it for others. When you change your energy, the energy between you and others changes. Bring in some understanding and learnings to the situation. See it from a higher perspective. Take the perspective of a neutral third party; as if you were someone else not emotionally involved in the situation. Understand that you sent off an energy that others tapped into but no more, never again will you allow that to happen. Tell the Universe now, right now, **"I'm doing things in a different way. I am a strong, powerful, capable person."**

Repeat that phrase with belief:

> ***"I'm doing things in a different way.***
> ***I am a strong, powerful, capable person."***

Don't just say it the once or twice, say it hundreds of times with meaning. Say it when you wake up in the morning, when you go to work, throughout the day and when you go to bed at night. Say it with commitment, strength and determination. Positivity will start to seep into your subconscious mind when you commit to it.

Feel free to use a phrase more personal to you if you wish but make it positive and powerful and commit to it. If you want the Universe to believe it you must too.

In childhood, and very often in adulthood, bullying usually involves a group with a ringleader. The group acts as sheep, just doing what the ringleader says. The ringleader hides behind the sheep and, without them, they are not so brave. This means you have a weak ringleader and weak sheep trying to find some power in their lives. It may be that they are part of the 'pack' just to feel safe and not be bullied themselves.

An eleven year old girl came to me over exam anxiety but after a couple of sessions she revealed to her mum and to me that she was being bullied at school. This was quite a shock to her mum but great that we were now aware of it as we could now address the situation.

This is what we did:

Her mum made the school aware of the bullying. We talked to the girl about bullies; how they were weak and when you stand up for yourself they back down. We also did some work around confidence. We did the Circle of Excellence.

We had an imaginary circle, which she was only allowed to stand in when she felt confident. I got her to connect with the feeling of confidence and to stand in the circle and continue to build her confidence. We then added some confidence music. The song I always think of is *'Rock DJ'* by Robbie Williams as I recall him strutting around in the video looking very confident.

Then I started to act the role of the bully so I would say something nasty to her like "hey four eyes" and she would step in and say "get lost, four eyes are better than two". It was important for her to give as good as she got and she did, with some guidance. We would turn up the confidence, she was imagining her confident song and we would practice the Circle of Excellence, building up her confidence.

Her school allowed her to play her confidence music on her MP3 player in break-time.

She also practiced her Circle of Excellence at home with her mum. By repeating the Circle of Excellence, she was building her confidence and reprogramming her subconscious. She was embedding in her subconscious the fact that confidence should be her behaviour now.

One way that the subconscious creates new habits is by repeating a behaviour or imagining the behaviour over and over. By repeating this confident behaviour and specifically by addressing the bullying situation, her subconscious was starting to believe she could and would stand up for herself.

A few weeks later her mum contacted me and told me that she told the bullies to *"f*ck off"* and had no more trouble from them. Since then she has really blossomed and has done amazing things.

Bullying can develop into a pattern in your life. I see it as an energy which we give off that says, *"I'm insecure, I lack self-esteem, I'm vulnerable, come bully me"*. The bullies will recognise and seize that energy. It's time to give off the *"I stand strong and I'm not to be messed with!"* energy.

Girls four years older than me, who went to my sister's school, bullied me when I was ten years old. These girls waited for me, as they knew I had to go past their school in order to get home.

When I went to secondary school and our year bully started on me, I quickly realised I needed to stand up for myself otherwise it was going to be five years of hell. I answered her back with the attitude of *'you don't scare me'* and guess what ….. she left me alone because she realised I was prepared to stand up for myself.

This wasn't natural for me to do but the more I stood up to any bullying type behaviour, the easier it got. It was as if I had developed an invisible cloak of protection, which covered up any fear and insecurity.

I then found myself defending others who she was trying to bully and even offered to fight her so she wouldn't pick on my friend. So I say *"Thank you!"* to the big girl bullies from my sister's school because you made me recognise the need to stand up for myself. I have more stories on bullies but they are for another time.

The way people treat you is very much related to the energy and attitude you give off, be Robbie in *'Rock DJ'* and strut your stuff.

Things to know about bullying:

- It has been reported that when you stand up to bullies for seven seconds they back down.
- The energy you give off is important. Strut your stuff. Rock your own DJ.
- You don't need to be one of the clique. Be okay with being you. Stand up for your beliefs and morals.
- If others don't accept the brilliant you, for your quirks and differences then it's *'their shit'* not yours!

- Don't be afraid to point out the other person's behaviour to them. Some may be shocked you have taken it that way, and may even be apologetic. Others will realise they've been found out and even be embarrassed about their behaviour. They may be defensive or tell you you've blown it out of proportion but that's 'their shit'. Ask them why they are speaking to you in that way but do it face to face.
- If someone is bullying then chances are they are insecure. They may have been bullied themselves. They may be jealous and they may feel you are better than them. That's all *'their shit'.* Don't be a sponge for their shit.
- Bullying is weak behaviour. Bullies are weaker than you. Are you going to allow yourself to be treated badly by someone weaker than you?

Don't seek victimhood

There is another issue with bullying; which is how do you define behaviour as bullying or boisterous, are people having fun or being direct? When someone has been bullied, they are more alert to bullying behaviour and sometimes struggle to separate bullying from assertiveness or other types of behaviour. It is as if their bullying radar is on high alert.

Perhaps the colleague who is assertive towards you, is assertive towards everyone. It may not be aggressive behaviour. Perhaps the people who laughed at you and poked fun thought it was just a bit of fun but if you feel they have taken it too far, give them an opportunity to stop by telling them, *"that's enough now, please give it a rest. I've had enough".* If they carry on then this may well be classed as bullying.

Keep things in perspective and remember, victimhood is a form of powerlessness, so you must change something. Don't be a sponge for other people's bad behaviour. Be comfortable being the wonderful you, weird you, quirky you, tall, thin, short, fat, unique you. The more comfortable you are with being you, the less likely others are going to bother you.

What can be classified as bullying?

Bullying does come in many forms. Often those who bully have not even registered their behaviour as bullying. Here are some examples of bullying behaviour:

- Constantly putting someone down.
- Messing with, hiding or destroying someone's belongings.
- Deliberately leaving someone out - by not inviting them on a night out or by making a drink for everyone else but them.
- Being intimidating.
- Anything physically or verbally aggressive.
- Constantly ignoring a particular person.
- Spreading lies and rumours about someone.
- Frequently criticising the person.
- Using social media to be aggressive, intimidating or belittling.
- Damaging a person's reputation by spreading malicious gossip or sharing personal information.
- Name calling or insulting. In particular being personal about the way someone looks, speaks or acts.
- Sharing photos of someone of a personal nature.

MANTRAS

"I am a strong and powerful person and I stand my ground."

"I am just as good as many and better than most."

16. Over-Analysing

*"It is over-analysing that causes uncertainty, not the
situations you are analysing. When you check in with how
you are at this precise moment, 99.9% of the time
you'll realise that all is fine."*

Ann Bowditch

Now let's look further into what goes on in the anxious mind and just how illogical it can be. One key difference between someone suffering anxiety and someone who doesn't is the level of analysing they do.

Here are some examples:

Example 1: You and your partner go out with a group of people. During the evening you make a comment, which you think has upset a friend. Your partner was involved in the same conversation but noticed nothing, goes to bed and has a great night's sleep. You were convinced that when you told your friend you preferred cats to dogs they were upset. You knew they were a dog lover and love their dog Fifi. Now you are chastising yourself for telling them you prefer cats. You wish you had never brought up the subject. You think they are upset with you, you run the conversation over and over in your mind imagining how it could have gone better. You also run through what might happen when you see them next and how they might react. You believe that they are annoyed with you. This keeps you awake for hours. You eventually drop off to sleep but awaken during the night and start thinking about the entire scenario again.

The Reality: Your friend did pull a face when you said you preferred cats but that's only because their preference is dogs. They respect the fact that you have a different preference to them. It's not like you said Fifi is the ugliest dog you ever saw, you just expressed a preference in general for cats, which you are fully entitled to do. It was not a big deal to your friend. They are sleeping soundly, not giving the conversation a second thought. When they see you next time they do not mention the previous conversation. In fact, they have forgotten it because it really is not important. It didn't matter to them *in the slightest* whether you prefer cats or dogs.

Example 2: You send your friend Sarah a text. Sarah usually replies within five minutes but over an hour has gone by and she hasn't replied. You start to think that Sarah is annoyed with you so you try to think of anything you have done which may have upset her. You think someone may have said something to her about you that isn't true and she believes them. You start to worry about Sarah, perhaps something bad has happened to her. You run through many possible scenarios as to why she hasn't responded.

The Reality: Sarah felt tired so put her phone on silent and went to bed early.

In the above scenarios the anxiety brain has been over-working, creating pantomimes, believing bad of you and ruining your peace of mind.

When we are in analysing mode, we are creating our own stories. We do not know what the other person is thinking or feeling or what is happening for them. We start to imagine conversations, consider worst-case scenarios because the mind thinks if it can deal with those situations then you'll be fine. When you have assessed the worst-case scenario, it causes you to worry more and possibly even panic. You then run through the possible ways of dealing with this imagined situation and this makes you even more anxious.

You have created an entire pantomime around an event that may not ever happen or is a complete fabrication of reality. You are creating all types of possibilities of events which will probably never happen. This thought process is ruining your peace of mind and keeping your body charged with adrenalin and cortisol.

This is the reality of it all:
- Most of the things you analyse over and over are just creations of your own imagination. They are not real – they are your very own pantomime.
- Most worst-case scenarios rarely happen and, if they do, it is

unlikely that they will happen in the way that you expect them to. They are just dramas of your own creation.

- You are far more resourceful than you give yourself credit for. This means that in the rare, and I mean very rare, event something bad does happen, you **will** deal with it. You **will** have help to deal with it and you **will** get through it.
- Over-analysing is not your friend, it is not serving you, it represents a big fabrication of reality.

Shit happens – no harm done

I recall a lovely client who suffered with anxiety. She was about to go on a short break away but was worried that during a meal out her baby would cry. She worried the crying would bother the other diners and they would think she was a bad mother.

Prior to her break she had had no problems with her baby when out, which would indicate she had no real reason to think he would cry. I reminded her that should he cry, then she had options and she could leave the restaurant. I also reminded her that we are all used to babies crying. I've been on many a plane journey hearing a screaming baby. Usually in such a situation people empathise with the parents, because we recognise they are probably stressed and trying to quieten the baby. This really is a "shit happens scenario". It's how you deal with it that matters. It is easy to apologise. In most situations it is possible to leave. No harm done. Usually an apology goes a very long way because people realise you are being respectful towards them.

Once people are out of the restaurant they will move on. The same as when we get off the plane, very rarely do any of us give the screaming baby a second thought. Shit happens. No harm done.

There are very few situations that you cannot resolve or remove yourself from. You would be amazed at what resources, skills and abilities you have when needed.

My client went out for meals on her break with her husband and baby and the baby was absolutely fine. All her worry was an imagined drama that didn't happen.

Having an active mind can be beneficial in many situations such as in business or if you are an engineer perhaps. Learning to calm the mind is important when analytical behaviour is taking away your peace.

Top Tips

When you find yourself analysing, ask: "Is this the truth or am I creating a pantomime?" Remind yourself to stay in the *now*.

Ask yourself: *"What is the best that could happen?"* Start to focus on the positive.

Most of the things you worry about are not going to happen, are insignificant in the great scheme of things and the only person fretting over them is you. If you are the only person fretting over them then chances are you are giving these things way too much attention.

Occasionally shit happens but it is how you deal with it that counts. Don't spend your life focussing on scenarios which haven't happened. Know that when real stress happens, you will deal with it, you will breathe through it and you are far more resourceful than you ever thought you were.

MANTRAS

"I have all the resources I need to deal with situations as and when they arise"

"My mind is at peace, in this moment all is well and I am calm."

17. The Inner Voice

**"Don't let the noise of others' opinions
drown out your own inner voice."**

Steve Jobs

We all have an inner voice. In fact, you could say, we all have a number of inner voices.

When someone suffers with anxiety, the inner voice is usually negative and goes through various scenarios of what might happen; the 'what ifs'. The inner voice can also be very critical of you, telling you that you 'aren't good enough' or 'can't cope' among many other negative comments.

You are not your thoughts!! The inner voice is the noise in your mind. It does not define you unless you allow it to. It does not control you unless you allow it to. As you start to become more aware of these thoughts, observing them as a third party, you will begin to dissociate yourself from such negative and unhelpful thoughts. You will begin to recognise them for what they are; the noise in your head and not the truth. You will no longer identify with that negativity and form a new, more positive and wonderful reality. This will mean that 'you' start to control your inner voice.

The quality of the inner voice can have a big impact on how we feel about ourselves, other people, activities and life in general.

It is important to address your inner voice. Firstly, we need to know what your inner voice is like. Here are a few questions to help decide:

1. Is your inner voice mostly positive or negative?
2. Does it put you down?
3. Does it remind you of someone else (eg a parent or teacher)?
4. Does it worry a lot?
5. Does it expect the worse to happen?
6. Do you wish it would stop talking sometimes?

Usually when someone suffers with anxiety, the inner voice is negative, worries a lot and expects bad things to happen. Very often it is self-critical too.

Here are a few examples of what the inner voice might be saying:

"What if that happens?"

"I'm useless"

"I can't do that"

"I can't cope"

"I'm scared"

"It's a disaster"

"What if I have a panic attack?"

Years ago I recognised my inner voice could sometimes be quite negative towards me. For example, if I dropped a glass, I would call myself "an idiot" or worse. I started to counter-act the negativity by saying "it's okay, everyone drops things, it's not the worst thing that could happen". My inner voice conversation would then go something like this:

(Drop glass)

"You idiot"

"It's ok, these things happen. It's not a major disaster" – this phrase immediately diluted the first response and took some of the negative energy out of it.

As time went on and I continued this process, I recognised I was being more positive about myself:

(Drop glass)

"These things happen. It's no big deal. Don't worry"

(The End)

The important point here is that I had stopped calling myself an 'idiot'!

The more often you connect with the inner voice by using it in a positive way, the more automatic positive behaviour becomes.

I started to cut out negativity about simple things, such as the weather or being stuck at traffic lights.

As a small and lightweight cyclist the wind was constantly more challenging for me than most and, living on an island, it was nigh on impossible to escape the wind. I could have thought *"I'm going to get blown all over the place here"* or *"I never go well in the wind"* but my trained positive inner voice would say *"the wind makes me a stronger rider"* or *"I'm good in tough conditions"* or *"everyone else is hating this weather and that gives me the mental edge".* Notice how much more empowering positivity is.

> **"If you think you can do a thing or think you can't do a thing, you're right."**
>
> *Henry Ford, Founder of the Ford Motor Company*

18. Ho'oponopono

"I'm Sorry
Please Forgive Me
I Love You
Thank You."

Now it gets deep. Lack of forgiveness keeps you stuck in the energy of an event. The inability or reluctance to forgive may keep you anxious, depressed or sick. It may stop your life moving on by keeping you and your energy stuck in the time the event happened.

When you get to a much higher level of enlightenment you will realise that there was nothing to forgive because everything that has happened in your life was as it was meant to be, even the parts you did not like, hated and wish you never had to experience. This includes the events that you really cannot, even now, understand why they happened. All those perceived negative events were building you up for something greater.

It's all just perfect. Not in the sense that it was easy or fun but it was all as it was meant to be. These experiences were leading you to a more enlightened place, giving you the opportunity to use these events as stepping stones of personal development and discovery. We grow and develop our inner wisdom when we go through tough times. Often it is those tough times which are a turning point in our lives. Without them we wouldn't gain those invaluable insights.

Ho'oponopono is a powerful Hawaiian Prayer for Forgiveness. It is also used as a clearing technique, which means you can use it on any issue you wish to clear such as, abandonment, trust, relationship issues and pretty much anything else. I have found the better aligned my energies are with the Universe the more successful the energy work I do.

This Hawaiian Prayer clears out unconscious thoughts, beliefs, and memories. As we continue self-development work, our energies synchronise with the energies of the Universe. We gain valuable insight into how life works and we accumulate wisdom. We carry less baggage around with us and we are able to achieve what we desire.

When seeking to attract something into your life do so for the good of many or all, not just for yourself. When we create for the benefit of others, we create a very positive energy that is in alignment with the Universe.

The energy of our thoughts, spoken words, actions, beliefs and behaviours go far wider than this. We must take responsibility for everything in our consciousness. When we do that, we can start to change the world which includes 'our inner world'. We change what we attract, the people we attract and how people respond to us.

One of the most amazing stories I have ever heard was of a Hawaiian therapist called Dr Ihaleakala Hew Len. Dr Len cured an entire ward of criminally insane patients without meeting any of them. This is the power of energy.

This is how he did it: Dr Len set up office in the hospital where the patients resided and reviewed each of their files in order to understand their crimes. By repeating Ho'oponopono, he worked on his beliefs and feelings about their crimes. The energy of Ho'oponopono was clearing away the negativity and creating new positive energy. Doing this through Ho'oponopono, he healed not just himself, but the patients too. This happens because, energetically, we are all connected. My website section includes a link so you can read about Dr Len.

This goes to show that we are all part of one consciousness and our thoughts, spoken words, beliefs and actions have widespread impact. This is amazing because you can create change within the Universe by creating positivity.

Start with positive thoughts, clear out your unhelpful beliefs, come from a place of love, remove your fears, make your actions loving ones, be kind and change the world. When you focus outward on how you, yes *you*, can make a positive difference to the world, then you give anxiety less energy and create beneficial energy for yourself. Of course thoughts must be followed by action.

If you are just reading about energy and spirituality for the first time, I understand this may be just a bit too 'out there' for you. Over time, as you continue to work on your self-development, you will come across more amazing stories and experiences and gain more wisdom and understanding. So right now it is okay for this to seem odd or uncomfortable to you.

We attract what we focus on. This is an aspect of quantum mechanics. Therefore if we focus on not being good enough we will be given many opportunities to confirm we are *not good enough.* However, if we put out there that we are capable, we have skills, abilities and other great things to offer the world, even if these aspects of ourselves are not fully developed yet, the energies of the Universe will start to acknowledge that to be our truth.

If you focus on fear, you will bring more fear energy into your life.
If you focus on peace, love and joy you will bring more of that
energy into your life.

"What you resist not only persists, but will grow in size"

Carl Jung

Our truth is linked to our individual perceptions of ourselves, other people and life. My truth is I am unsociable and quirky, how I see life is a result of my own perceptions and I create my reality. What's your truth? Self-reflection is a great way to gain wisdom.

Ho'oponopono turns things on their head. The power of the Prayer is in the feeling of liberation from unhelpful emotions and in the willingness of the Universe to let go, recognise that there never was anything to forgive and bring in love. Love is the greatest energy of all.

As the Prayer goes:

I'm Sorry
Please Forgive Me
I Love You
Thank You

Let's break this down into understanding the individual aspects of this Prayer:

I'm Sorry

I'm sorry I judged you. I recognise I am not a victim. I never was a victim. I am in a learning process for my greater good and the good of all. Your actions reminded me of pain. Your actions resulted in me feeling pain. I'm sorry I thought this was your fault. I am sorry something such as this has happened within my consciousness and therefore I take responsibility for it. I have the power to liberate myself from pain for me, for you, for everyone, now and always, to release pain for the greater good. I have much to gain from this experience. I judged you, I apologise, I am sorry.

Please Forgive Me

Please forgive me for judging you. I misunderstood our soul contract. You loved me so much that you would take that action for me. You lovingly brought me to this point guiding me to insights and learnings I could not have otherwise experienced without your direction. I bring the learnings and understandings to my consciousness for healing. I have the power to heal. Forgive me for disturbing you. Please forgive me.

I Love You

You loved me so much that you would do that act. You would allow yourself to be seen as the 'bad' person. I recognise my soul has done that for you when our soul paths have crossed over time. I love that you brought this to my attention. I love and accept you unconditionally. I love and accept myself unconditionally. I see the divine in you. I love you.

Thank You

Thank you for everything you have done for me. Thank you for bringing this to my consciousness to clear for all of us. Thank you for helping me to learn, to grow, to heal, to let go. Thank you for leading me further on this incredible journey and teaching me forgiveness. Thank you for teaching me to step into my power and use that power wisely. I recognise I am a powerful divine being of light. Thank you for everything. Thank you.

Summary

When you embrace Ho'oponopono, it is a powerful technique, which you can use on any issue whenever you are feeling blocked. All you need to do is decide on the issue you wish to clear and repeat the four line Prayer over and over again.

It can help to score the emotion related to an event from zero to ten and then after repeating Ho'oponopono a few times, check on the score.

As I've mentioned, it's ok for this to seem odd or uncomfortable. If Ho'oponopono is not for you right now, that's fine too.

19. My Shit – Your Shit

**"Not one drop of my self-worth depends
on your acceptance of me."**

Quincy Jones

Shit happens and at times life will throw you curveballs but it is how you deal with these curveballs that is important. The same goes for those you come into contact with such as friends, family and colleagues.

Many of us take on other people's shit so **STOP IT!** Deal with *your shit* and let others deal with *their shit*. It's that simple.

Here is a list of the type of things I categorise as "other people's shit":-

1. Anything they constantly moan about. While they are moaning they are not addressing *their shit*. Don't be the sponge for their negativity because they are too lazy or afraid to address *their shit.*

2. They do not like your actions and criticise you. As long as you act with good intent and do not deliberately upset anyone then if someone does react negatively to something you have said or done, it is, *their shit.* This means your actions have triggered something within them but it is important to recognise this is about them, not you. It is quite simply *their shit.* This may be particularly relevant if you are changing your ways, becoming more confident or stepping into your power.

3. You may be asked to an event but not want to go so you say "no thanks" to the invitation. This response may upset them but it is *their shit.* You didn't sign a contract to go to every event they have asked you to, did you?

4. You go out for a meal and don't want to drink alcohol or eat a dessert. Why on earth does what you drink or eat have anything to do with anyone else? Sometimes you feel you will offend someone. Well, this is a classic case of *their shit.* If you fall into this trap you need to get a grip of it. There are ways

of saying no thank you in a polite manner. You have a mind of your own for a good reason.

5. They need a loan because they have spent all their money on a big holiday. Take a guess whose *shit it is*? Yes, it's theirs. They made the decision to spend their money on the holiday. Just because you are better at looking after your money or earn more, do not feel obligated to sort their life out.

6. You do not immediately respond to emails, phone calls or texts. You don't have to respond immediately and if someone expects you to then it is clearly *their shit*.

None of this means you do not have to be a good friend. You can still listen, be empathetic, compassionate and all the things you want to be but don't be pulled into others' negativity and do not feel responsible for them. Set boundaries for yourself. These boundaries protect you. Do not let others overstep those boundaries. If you do not set those, all-important, boundaries then you will make yourself vulnerable to absorbing too much negativity and being 'put upon'.

What makes you so great?

There is an amazing phrase from the enlightened Melissie Jolly, creator of Colour Mirrors, that goes: *"What makes you think you are more divine than someone else that you have to do that for them?"*

Put in other words: *"If you keep on bailing people out or doing things for them they will never learn to do those things for themselves or work out how to resolve their own mistakes or problems".* Have you ever considered your actions of saving others may have stopped someone learning, improving, growing or even excelling?

Let's say, for example, you keep giving your grown up child money because they are constantly overspending. Why do you think they haven't learned to act responsibly with money? It's because you keep bailing them out.

Perhaps you are the person who has to save everyone. Wherever there is a crisis there you are putting things right, saving the world.

Of course the world needs saviours but are you taking on too much? Is this behaviour draining you of your energy and causing stress? Are you feeling pulled in too many directions? If so, recognise this is the life you have created for yourself and because you created it, you can change it.

Do not always be the one to jump in and save a situation. You can still pass on your best wishes and even help out but draw a line on where your responsibility stops. You are not just helping yourself by taking a step back, you are also helping others take responsibility for themselves.

Here's what you can do:

Recognise where you have been taking on other people's shit and quite simply start to apply the *"My Shit – Your Shit"* rule.

If they react to anything you say or do in a negative way recognise it is *their shit.* You have done nothing wrong. It is not up to you to sort their life out. You are under no contract to do what they want you to do or act how they want you to act.

If you are about to get dragged into some drama ask yourself a few questions:

- Where might this lead?
- How involved do I want to get?
- Am I prepared to deal with the possible consequences of getting involved?
- By me becoming involved, what am I stopping this person from learning, doing or achieving?
- Is this *my shit*?

If you feel you are about to get sucked into something that doesn't feel right, you need to apply the *"My Shit – Your Shit"* rule.

If you are feeling judged, you must apply the *"My Shit – Your Shit"* rule.

If you feel others are creating negative energy around you, time to apply the *"My Shit – Your Shit"* rule.

If others criticise the new wonderful you, you definitely must apply the *"My Shit – Your Shit"* rule.

20. Perfectionism

"Strive for continuous improvement, instead of perfection."

Kim Collins

Perfection is a misconception. What is perfect for one person may not be perfect to another. We are perfect in our imperfections. You could say we are imperfectly perfect or perfectly imperfect. This world was never meant to be perfect, we were never meant to be perfect. If that was the case then we would all be robots. If you are trying to be perfect for you, for someone else or for some other reason, free yourself because your perfectionism behaviour is taking away your enjoyment of life.

When you die would you like your obituary to say: *"J Bloggs was perfect and did everything perfectly throughout their life"?* The obituary would probably go on to say *"They lived a miserable life because being perfect wasn't easy, they were unable to relax, they were hard on themselves, they were never ever satisfied with the way they looked, anything they did and the way things turned out but at least they were perfect".* That is what striving for perfection gets you.

Constantly striving for perfection is telling your subconscious mind that something is wrong, constantly wrong. If I was striving for perfection, I would have probably never written this book or embarked on just about every challenge I have done in life. I would never have been perfect enough to race my bike, be a personal trainer or be a therapist.

We live in a society which seeks out perfection, resulting in people having botox, surgery and other procedures to look better. Teenagers are stressed because they are not getting the perfect grades or being perfect enough for their friends. I know of a teenager who was told by her classmates that she was too fat so she lost weight and then was told she was too thin. In a few months she had developed a serious eating disorder and her self-esteem was at rock bottom. If someone tells you that you are too fat it's *their shit.* If they say you are too thin, it's *their shit.* Do not change for someone else. Only change for yourself, for your own good.

This focus on perfectionism leaves people feeling inferior, depressed, incapable and dissatisfied. Social media has not been our friend by putting down those who do not fit into the 'perfect' category and then criticising those who make changes in that bid for perfection.

You cannot win in the eyes of the media but you can win in your own eyes. We have seen a fighting back from some areas of society, creating a focus on self-acceptance but there is still a conflict out there in the media and in our own lives.

Achieving perfection is the biggest misconception of all. Your attempt to achieve perfection will sap your energy, your happiness, pleasure and your life. Let it go. Why does perfectionism matter anyway? Who does it matter to? So what if your house is a bit messy, so what if you wear scruffy clothes, so what if you look like you have been dragged through a bush backwards. If it doesn't matter to you then it doesn't matter. If it does matter then why?

What is more important is what is in your heart and in your head, how you treat people, animals and the earth and whether you act with integrity. Why does anything else matter so much?

Let go of any need to be perfect for anyone, just be imperfect you and do that perfectly. In fact if you have always strived for perfection, I dare or challenge you to deliberately be imperfect for a day. Feel the freedom of imperfection. Go out without make up on, lounge around in your pyjamas or leave a mug on the table. Do something you wouldn't do. Embrace your uniqueness, your quirkiness and your imperfections. Be uniquely, amazing, fantastic you because that is what you are and who you are.

21. Challenges of Life

*"Challenges are what make life interesting;
overcoming them is what makes life meaningful."*

Joshua J Marine

You were born with everything you needed to come onto this planet. It may be that not all of your gifts are apparent or fully formed yet, which means that there is more to explore as your understanding, skillset and knowledge expands.

It is the challenges in life that make us complete. What you saw as mistakes were just learning curves, what you saw as disasters were experiences that helped you become the fully-formed and wonderful you.

You could only know what it is like to feel vulnerable by experiencing vulnerability. You could only understand betrayal by being betrayed. You have learnt the feeling of fear by experiencing something frightening. These can be turned into gifts for you.

These emotions are all part of the human experience and we can put a tick next to the feelings you've had and say, *"I've experienced that, but I don't need to keep being in that moment, I don't need to keep reliving the vulnerability, the betrayal or feeling scared. Thanks for the learning, thanks for the experience. Now I need to let go and step into my power. I am putting my energy into being the best version of myself I can be, which starts with living for now."*

I could not be the therapist I am now without the challenges I have had in life. I would not have the empathy I have with people on many levels were it not for the events in my life. I did not understand why I was going through those events at the time but now I understand they were part of a bigger picture. I have felt powerless, lonely, isolated, let down, insignificant, angry and many other feelings through life experiences.

You may not understand why you have suffered or feel sad, angry, lonely or depressed but they are part of your unique story. You have choices as to whether you stay in those emotions, but you are doing yourself a disservice if you let those past events take charge of your future life.

As you continue to learn, explore and embrace life, you will develop a higher level of understanding if you open your mind and heart to this. If you close yourself off to it then you will carry on as you are and miss out on all that is possible.

Here are some examples of my life challenges:

- My sister was born with a cleft lip and palate, which presented a number of difficulties for my family. She was badly bullied at school. This gave me great empathy. I would never tease anyone for their differences, difficulties or challenges. I would stand up for people who were not confident enough to stand up for themselves. This made me a better person than I might have been had this not been part of my life experience. It also gave me a healthy curiosity about other people's struggles that no doubt enables me to help others.
- I failed the 11-Plus. I also failed to be selected for the Island under-16 hockey team on my first attempt. When we experience failure, we appreciate our successes more. Perhaps those failures also led to me being more determined in various areas of my life such as my sport and career.
- I have had many experiences where I have felt let down. This causes me to look at myself as these 'let down' experiences help me to let go of emotional baggage and continue my journey of personal development.

EXERCISE – Don't Skip It!

1. Make a note of the challenging, even awful, events in your life.
2. Look for the gifts, the positive elements, within your experiences and write them down. Use these questions to help you.
    - What did they enable you to do?
    - What did you learn?
    - What emotions did each event enable you to experience?
    - How did this contribute to your personal growth?
3. How can you use that experience in a positive way in the future? This may be on a personal level or to help others.

22. Be Positive

"The Positive Thinker Sees the Invisible, Feels the Intangible, and Achieves the Impossible."

Sir Winston Churchill

To be positive will make such a difference to your energy, how you see life, the world, how you interact with others, the energy you give off, the people you attract in your life, how you deal with situations, how the cells of your body react and consequently your health and well-being. Being positive will help you in every area of your life.

I had a lovely lady come to see me. She always saw the negative in every situation. Life was a catastrophe waiting to happen. She had experienced upsets in her life, as we all do, but her current life was pretty good with children, a good husband, a fulfilling job; all the things most people want in their lives.

Her belief system was very negative, based around a belief of *'things will be hard'*. Every time something bad did happen it was just a confirmation of *'life is hard'*. Those challenging situations confirmed her belief. *'Bad things happen and there's no point being happy because right around the corner disaster will strike.'*

She was focusing on the negative and missing all the positives in her life, of which there were many. Her whole demeanour matched her negative energy. Even her smile was more of a wince.

I'm not sure how you feel reading this but as I type this, I can feel my energy sinking and the life being sucked out of me.

You can find doom and disaster in all areas of life if you are focused on them. You can notice the dark clouds and rain or you can see the green hillsides, rainbows, patches of blue sky and sunshine.

I'm not asking you to be happy all the time but put a positive spin on things. Know that even when you are going through the darkest of times in your life, at the end of the tunnel there is light. When you have a negative thought, add a positive thought to even things up.

I don't like the rain but when it does rain I tell myself how lucky we are to have the rain. The plants will get watered and we won't have a hosepipe ban. It hasn't changed the fact I don't like the rain but I focus on the benefits, which makes it difficult to be depressed about the rain.

Most importantly be kind to yourself. Don't look for the negatives about yourself, look for the positives as there are plenty of good things to focus on. You are perfect as you are because you are how you were meant to be. Those personality quirks are just fine, the physical bits you don't like about yourself are not important, you are constantly evolving so do that in the most positive way you can. Think of all the things you have done well, the skills you have learned, the talents you have and the challenges you have overcome. Focus on those, be honest with yourself, don't have grey-tinted glasses, have rose-tinted glasses!

I love my feet and I love to tell people how amazing my feet are. I have beautiful feet. It's a running joke amongst a few close friends. I have no bunions and no hard skin. They are pretty damn awesome feet! They are so damn awesome I am tempted to include a picture in this book. In fact at one time a picture of my feet was my screensaver on my phone.

As I said, this feet-worshipping is mainly done in jest but even so, I have developed for myself a reputation for having lovely feet. Others may not be so impressed with my feet but I really don't care.

Find a part of your body you love, absolutely any part of your body, and love it like you have never loved it before. It can be your index finger or the palm of your hand, your neck, or your left ear. It really doesn't matter. Be positive about yourself, every aspect of yourself. By doing this you are creating good energy for yourself.

Positivity is your friend, the cells of your body are listening to everything; every thought, everything you say, everything others say to you. Put positive healthy energy into your body and reap the rewards. The more you do this, the less fuel you give to negativity and worries.

Be loving and kind to others but be loving and kind to yourself first and foremost.

Start listening to your inner voice, that running commentary you have throughout the day, and notice where it is being unkind, negative or dismissive especially towards yourself. Bring in the positivity, humour, love and acceptance. It will change your world.

Here's what you can do:

- Be aware of your inner voice and be sure to put a positive spin on things.
- Turn events into the positive. Do not get sucked into negative conversations. If someone starts to pull on the negativity, put a positive spin on things. See this as a fun challenge. Help others see the positives in life too.
- Be with people who make you laugh, feel good and give you positive experiences.
- Laugh, laugh and laugh. Laughter is one hell of a medicine and reduces stress hormones. Laughter also boosts production of antibody-producing cells creating a more robust immune system. How fab is that?
- Recognise those negative thoughts or comments common to you and change them.

Let positivity become a way of life and soon you will realise how good your life is. How you see your life is down to you.

23. Remember 'Now'

"Life is lived in the present and directed toward a future."

Milton H. Erickson

In a sense you only have now. The past is a memory which you continue to give energy to and the future is a mental projection which you also give energy to. By focusing on either of these, you are missing something great and wonderful, you are missing **now**, this moment, because the only thing we really have and can be sure of is this moment. In a blink this moment has gone so grasp it with all of your attention, heart, energy and life.

Imagine time did not exist, there was no past and no future, there really only was now. How would you live your life differently if there were neither past nor future?

The past has its place in your life. It is part of your learning, part of what formed you as the person you are today and part of what contributed to your story. You will benefit the most when you utilise the past in the most positive way, by understanding events you considered bad or awful were experiences of life that have given you the knowledge and tools and learning you now have today.

So many people are grateful for the challenges they have had in their lives because they have come through them, out of the dark tunnel, into the light. Often those challenges have pushed them to do what they truly came onto this earth to do. There are so many examples of this.

Remember too that you have positive memories and those can be held in your heart and in your energy field and projected into the now and the future. You can use these positive memories as a springboard to create more positivity.

In reality, the future has to take some place in our mind but we need to focus on the future we want to have, on the person we desire to be, and work towards that. If you want to get a promotion, you must focus on what you need to do to get a promotion; that is a positive future focus. If you want to feel happy and enjoy life, you must focus on the feelings you want and apply your energy to those.

It is good and it is wonderful to give the future some of your focus because much of what you do now has an impact on your future. What you do 'now' can give you a better future. You could sit at home reflecting on all your worries or you can read this book and read it again and again so that the messages sink in. You could make notes about the key learnings from this book and you could action the exercises set in this book to create that future.

Whenever your awareness becomes distracted by the past or the future for negative reasons, you are blocking your innate ability to flourish and enjoy this moment.

If you have a negative emotional trigger then work towards releasing it, use the techniques in this book. You may be amazed that, by removing the negative emotion from events, you really can move on in your life.

We live in a truly amazing world. We were given senses so that we could experience it fully yet we bypass the greatest things about life because we don't have time or are too self-focused. Take a little time out of each day and appreciate something about the world we live in. I love to watch my cats. It doesn't matter what they are doing at the time. They could be sleeping, playing or eating. When I am watching them they bring me so much joy. What brings you joy?

This morning I did my first run on the cliffs for around 18 months. I just love our cliffs here in Guernsey, it is where I feel most at peace. While I did some stretches after the run looking out across the sea, I remembered how *at one* I felt with our gorgeous cliffs and how I had missed that feeling. I so love running on the cliffs, not necessarily for the discomfort I endure when running up steps but for being in touch with nature and being able to look out at such gorgeous views. When I am there I am in the moment, experiencing the wonders and beauty, peace and unity with the earth and nature.

When I am running, I will often remind myself to look out across the bays and see the tremendous views. The peaceful time while I am stretching, having accomplished my run, feels wonderful. My mind feels clearer and I am full of gratitude.

When you are in a moment of deep connection to the planet nothing else matters. All the worries, all the events that have happened to you, everything from the past and future literally do not exist right now, because *you are present, in the moment.* Breathe into it. There are no worries when you are truly there in the moment. When you allow yourself to let go you break free from chains of past-thinking and start to feel the freedom of life, **breathe in the now.** Be in this moment, be at peace in this moment. Right here, right now, you're okay.

In this state of deep connection, you take your mind to another place and life starts to fall into place. Positive thoughts, opportunities, beliefs and many other wonderful attributes are triggered from that deep connection with the Universe. It centres you, in many ways it is unexplainable but it takes your mind and energy to a different place.

EXERCISE – Don't Skip It!

Take yourself to a place where you can get in touch with nature; a park, nature trail or beach and see what you can notice. Use as many of your senses as possible. If you live near a beach, take your shoes off and paddle your feet in the water. This is a fantastic way to ground yourself. If you have a safe piece of ground to walk on, take your socks and shoes off and feel the earth under your feet. At the very least, do this twice a week but ideally daily.

Importantly, do not assume that this is unimportant. It may be the most important thing you do in a day so give it the priority you deserve.

EXERCISE – Don't Skip It!

Do the things listed below. These may appear simple but do not ignore them because they seem too easy. Very often it is the easy things which can create great changes.

- *Listen* to your own breath and appreciate being given life.
- *Touch* the trees and feel their bark.
- *Look* at the sky and experience vastness.
- *Feel* the breeze against your face.
- *Dip* your foot in the water.
- *Listen* to the birds sing.
- *Smell* the flowers and appreciate their beauty.
- *Stop* and notice all the wonders around you.
- *Watch* the moon and stars at night and be in touch with the Universe.
- *Taste* the fruit and bless the food available to you.

24. The High Vibe of Gratitude

"What we see depends mainly on what we look for."

John Lubbock

If you have done any self-development work in the past then you most likely will have come across the suggestion to bring gratitude into your life.

Everything is energy and the energy we give out tends to come back at us, which is why it is far better to have as much positivity in your life as possible.

Gratitude is such an easy way to achieve positive energy. Every night I think of three things I am grateful for. It does not matter if I am grateful for the same things two nights in a row, the important thing here is the *energy* of gratitude. Under the Law of Attraction, being grateful for the things you want in your life can bring more of those things to you.

Gratitude can be anything. I am grateful for my husband, my cats, my clients, my life, the sun, the rain, living on the lovely island of Guernsey and, of course, my lovely feet. I am grateful for the skills I have, colour, knowledge, fun, the tutors I've had, laughter and freedom. I truly am grateful for these things. It is important to feel the gratitude. There are so many things to be grateful for. The list is endless.

You don't need to write them down, you could just think of them. However, I find writing them down at the end of the day gives me a commitment on a daily basis to focus on what I am thankful for. It also helps to end the day with some good energy no matter how the day went.

It makes you feel better to be able to take a positive from events in your life which were unpleasant and place some gratitude on those experiences. I can look back at events in my life, which, at the time, were really not great to downright awful, but can take the positive from them. When you get into the gratitude mind-set you start to see the positives in those challenging situations. Those situations so often represent a key point of change in our lives. It is often when we reach the lowest point that we take action, either to seek help or take another path.

Perhaps those events led you to make a decision that would improve your life forever. Very often using these experiences to help others can also be very rewarding.

One of the biggest inspirations in current times is the acid attack victim Katie Piper. I use the term 'victim' rather loosely here because this woman has been a huge inspiration to many. She lost the sight in one eye following the attack and had numerous operations. Katie bravely made her plight public and brought this issue to the media's attention. She is a best-selling international author, inspirational speaker and TV presenter. Katie also set up her own charitable organisation called the Katie Piper Foundation.

Perhaps a name you are less familiar with but will become more aware of as people catch up with modern holistic health is Harry Massey. Harry suffered from severe Chronic Fatigue Syndrome for seven years leaving him bedridden. Harry had tried just about every kind of conventional and alternative healing approach in a bid to heal but to no avail. In his sick bed, rather than focusing on himself, Harry considered how he could create a health system that was natural and helped the body to heal itself.

Together with Peter Fraser, Harry created the Total WellNES System which provides a complete system to restore health and energy at its source. This system is blooming and I believe is only going to become a stronger and stronger force. As people today now want to take charge of their health and have had enough of putting nasty substances into their bodies, which can create other side-effects. I believe this system has a very bright future. Without his health issues, would Harry have co-created this innovative health system? Possibly not, and what a loss to society and modern health advancement that would have been. I am a practitioner of this system also referred to as NES Health.

Gratitude helps turn a negative into a positive and creates good energy. Gratitude is seeking the gift in life and the gift in your experiences then placing your focus on that.

EXERCISE – Don't Skip It!

Write a list of 10 things you are grateful for.

Each day, morning or night, write down three things you are grateful for.

Seek the gratitude from situations.

MANTRAS

"I am grateful for my calming breath"

"I am grateful for these new learnings"

"I am grateful that I have choices in life"

"I am grateful for my peaceful mind"

25. Bare Those Feet

"The earth has music for those who listen."

Unknown

The term 'grounding' (or 'earthing') has become something of a buzz-word. Nevertheless it is important to our mental and physical health and well-being and therefore must continue to be recognised for its immense benefits. In terms of anxiety, grounding can be hugely beneficial.

To a great extent the stress and anxiety people experience results from a disconnection between mind, body and earth. By being better connected in these areas, you will experience less stress and anxiety.

The interchangeable terms *earthing* and *grounding* refer to the act of walking barefoot on the earth. This allows the transfer of free electrons from the earth into your body, through the soles of your feet.

When we are disconnected from the earth our bodies do not hold a negative charge effectively. Our brains are also less effective and therefore the communication between mind and body becomes compromised. Our brains function much more effectively when our electrical systems works better.

Signs of being ungrounded

Mental signs:

* Anxious
* Over-thinking
* Constant worrying
* Feeling spaced out or absent-minded
* Easily distracted
* Over-dramatic

<u>Physical signs:</u>

- Poor sleep/insomnia
- Inflammation
- Chronic pain
- Fatigue
- Poor circulation

Grounding can help to reverse the damage caused by electro-magnetic fields (EMFs) and other types of radiation from Wi-Fi, mobile phones, computers and other damaging technology.

Another benefit is that grounding reduces inflammation. When our bodies are positively charged, the blood is thick and the cells of our bodies are trying to battle against free radicals. Grounding puts the body in its preferred state of being, which is slightly negatively charged. This alleviates inflammation as the blood becomes thinner. Grounding is a key component in the foundation of good health and well-being.

I used to have a very unsettling feeling through my body. The best way to describe it was like an electrical current going through parts of my body, especially my limbs. Once I started to ground myself this disappeared and I had a greater feeling of well-being.

There are many reported benefits to grounding which include:

- Reduces emotional stress
- Elevates mood
- Improves sleep
- Increases energy
- Helps support adrenal health function
- Improves feeling of wellness
- Reduces inflammation
- Reduces chronic pain
- Relieves muscle tension and headaches
- Alleviates symptoms of menstrual cycle

- Aids and often speeds up healing
- Reduces jet lag symptoms
- Protects the body from the effects of EMFs
- Decreases recovery time from injury
- Reduces snoring
- Normalises biological rhythms
- Normalises blood pressure and blood flow

There are different methods for grounding and I encourage you to try these out.

Barefoot Walking

Our ancestors used to walk around barefoot, which means they were always grounded. This suggests being ungrounded is a symptom of modern living. By grounding through direct contact with the earth, we can reinstate our body to its natural state of a slight negative charge. Barefoot walking helps us to absorb the nutrients of the earth. The very best place to do this is to walk on the beach and paddle your feet in the water. Water is a great conductor of energy.

Another method for grounding is to walk on grass. When walking barefoot, please be careful to ensure you are walking in a safe place away from anything and anywhere that could cause injury.

Bathing

Nothing beats a swim in the sea for grounding and the impact on your well-being. Alternatively bathing or using a foot spa containing Epsom salts or Himalayan salts is a lovely relaxing way to ground yourself.

Grounding Mat or Sheet

A grounding (or earthing) mat can be used under your feet while using a computer, which reduces your vulnerability to the EMFs. Many grounding mats come with a wrist strap option.

Note: when using grounding mats while working on computers, if your computer is plugged in, you may create a positive charge. To avoid this you should ensure your computer is not plugged in, therefore only ground yourself when the computer is working in battery mode. In my experience MacBooks are best unplugged when working on them in any event.

My preference is a grounding bed sheet because I have found greater benefit to this than the grounding mat. A sheet provides a fantastic eight hours of grounding while sleeping. To get the most benefit you would need to be naked, or mostly naked, so your skin is in contact with the sheet. It is worth buying a quality grounding sheet.

Use your Imagination

I'm sure by now you do not need me to explain that your mind is a powerful piece of kit and visualisation is very powerful.

Sit or lie and imagine your feet are like tree roots, connected to the earth and absorbing the earth's nutrients. Next imagine a connection between the crown of your head and the Universe. Connect with the Universal energy, imagine this being a beam of light and then send it through each of your chakras; the crown, third eye, throat, heart, solar plexus, sacral and base chakras down your body through your legs and feet and into the ground. Bring the earth's energy back up through your feet, legs and back through the chakras and then spreading out through your body to your aura. Spend at least five minutes doing this.

Information on Chakras

Chakras are energy vortexes throughout the body. Energy flows through these chakras. There are seven main chakras, which are those listed above. These chakras can become blocked or be too open, which can cause various types of disruption and disharmony in body, mind and spirit. It is possible to balance your chakras. You can do specific treatment for chakras, which is beyond the scope of this book.

Here are brief specifics on these seven chakras:

Root Chakra

- Location: Base of spine – tailbone area.
- Relates to: Survival issues, such as finances, feeling safe, food and courage.
- Colour: Red.

Sacral

- Location: Lower abdomen, about two inches below the navel and two inches inwards towards the body.
- Relates to: Trauma, creativity and sexuality.
- Colour: Orange.

Solar Plexus

- Location: Upper abdomen.
- Relates to: Self-esteem, self-confidence and will power.
- Colour: Yellow.

Heart

- Location: Centre of the chest just above the heart.
- Relates to: Love – giving and receiving.
- Colour: Green.

Throat

- Location: Throat.
- Relates to: Communication, self-expression, trust and truth.
- Colour: Blue.

Third Eye

- Location: Forehead between the eyes.
- Relates to: Wisdom, intuition and making decisions.
- Colour: Indigo.

Crown

- Location: Top of the head.
- Relates to: Connection to spirituality and bliss.
- Colour: Violet.

26. Creativity and Passion

"When you are being creative you lose yourself in the moment and at the same time embark on a process of finding yourself."

Ann Bowditch

Creativity is often overlooked as not being important in our lives, something we don't have time for. Some people pass themselves off as "not creative" which is something I used to do until I realised that creativity comes in many forms.

Some of the most amazingly creative people in the world release their traumas and innermost darkest thoughts through their creativity, such as painting, writing, making music or in some other creative way.

The benefits of spending some time being creative have ripple effects on your health and well-being. Creativity is known to help heal the sacral chakra, which is where we hold our trauma.

This seems like the perfect time to bring some colour in. Orange is the colour of the sacral chakra and the colour of trauma. The flip side of this is when you move out of the trauma the orange can bring bliss. The colour of creativity is turquoise. Turquoise is being in the flow, trust, faith, embracing movement and change. Think of the sea, just flowing easily and effortlessly. How does it make you feel to be near the sea or by a lake? For most of us it brings good feelings, perhaps peace and a feeling of connection with nature and life itself. Turquoise is also the colour of the higher heart centre, again moving us into love and positive energy.

I became a Colour Mirrors Practitioner in 2014 and Teacher in 2015. Colour Mirrors is a system made from coloured oils and essences which are stored in bottles. The word 'mirror' means a reflection of you, your life journey, emotions, experiences, what you are going through right now and many other aspects of you and your life.

This process acts at a subconscious level and people are usually amazed at just how perfect the bottles they have chosen are to the issue being addressed. Each bottle has wording to reflect the energy of that bottle and this wording can be incredibly powerful and guide you to continue your journey of personal development.

Colour Mirrors has opened my mind to new understandings and helped me hugely in my work. I even decorated my house to become a colour house painted in all sorts of colours and displaying many Colour Mirrors bottles. My favourite room is my Starlight Being room of Magenta and Gold. It has such a warm feel to it, so cosy and welcoming. My cats love it too. My staircase is multi-coloured, my living room pink of Starlight Love and so on.

The Starlights are a range of bottles made by the creator of the Colour Mirrors (CM) system, Melissie Jolly, at the request of my teacher, Korani. Although they are not a formal part of the CM set, I have experienced them as particularly powerful and enlightening. The bottles and the associated wording together are quite something to be experienced. To quote my teacher, Korani: *"The Starlights as a whole encompass many different qualities such as peace, freedom, joy, connection, radiance but overall, this set opens the way to simplify our lives, open to the beauty of everything and everyone in our world and guide us to the deeper, higher truths of the Universe".*

I had so much pleasure from re-decorating and selecting decorative items to go with the changes. Even my husband has said he really loves the changes and gains pleasure from the different coloured rooms.

Do not underestimate the value to your well-being of creating an environment that makes you feel good. Some of my rooms make me feel energised, others calm, but every single room makes me feel good in some way. Some re-decoration, fresh organisation and de-cluttering can give your living space, and therefore your mood, a great lift.

You may wonder what benefit this can have on anxiety but what if having a nicely decorated living environment or bedroom gives you a greater feel-good factor? That could be another one per cent or ten per cent to feeling better and improving your overall mood and therefore well-being. It doesn't have to cost a lot to make some simple changes which can lighten your mood.

Decorating your house is just one way of being creative. You may like to write or play music, sew, knit, colour, paint, write poems, cook, create woodwork or make jewellery; the opportunities for being creative are endless.

When you are being creative you get lost in what you are doing, the concept of time vanishes and you are completely engrossed in your project. During this time your subconscious is doing some valuable processing. This reminds me very much of something else... the state of trance. When in a trance, our subconscious has the ability to work through solutions, even if we are not aware that is happening. It is as if we give it an opportunity to be creative without the over analysing of the conscious mind.

Creativity has been used as a way to heal trauma for as long as we have known. It is ingrained within us but we get caught up in modern life and don't prioritise it the way that we should. Consider some of our greatest musicians and artists, most of them had some sort of demons to overcome, whether they had a traumatic childhood, or mental health or emotional issues. As I said, creativity is naturally deeply ingrained in us. We know innately how to look after ourselves but our modern day living and busy lifestyles have dampened this intuition.

To give yourself the overall good mental health you need, you may need to make some practical lifestyle changes to enable time for these valuable well-being tools.

What would you be doing if you didn't have a television? Most likely you would spend more time with nature and more time being creative. Take an evening without the television and see where it leads you.

When I look back through my life I find elements of creativity. As a teenager I created scrap books of pop stars or sports stars from cutting out bits from magazines. I've created tapestries and used them to make cushions. I have made jewellery and given my house a facelift. To look at these areas of creativity it would be fair to think I had a creative streak but I assure you I do not. I may not be the next Picasso or Lady Gaga but it doesn't matter. What does matter is I find a special headspace where I'm in another place while being creative. I also get satisfaction from seeing the finished product. Let your creativity bring you joy and peace of mind. Creativity really is a gift.

It is never too late to try something new. My husband and I learned to kart at 44 years old. My husband learned the guitar when he was 46 years old. I changed career once aged 38 and then again at 41 years old. Don't ever use the *"I'm too old"* excuse, because it's not true. There are people running marathons in their eighties or even nineties.

I believe we all have passion in us for something. For some it is music, others it may be sport, work or charity work. I love animals too, especially cats and another passion of mine is to help out at our local Animal Aid as a kitty-cuddler. What are your passions?

EXERCISE – Don't Skip It!

I challenge you:

1. Take at least one evening out a week to be creative.
2. Create something you can feel proud of.
3. Find more creative ways of doings things.
4. If you don't have a passion then start to explore.
5. Declutter your home, car and workplace.
6. Bring more colour into your life.

SECTION 3
EXERCISES

We will now move through to the bulk of the exercises. These can be done in any order. Some exercises may be more relevant at any given time.

If you would like to book any sessions with me please contact me directly at hypnotherapy@suremail.gg or ann@hypnotherapy.gg or via my website www.hypnotherapy.gg

27. Breathing

Breathing does sound like the most simple thing to do. By breathing deeply, you are not only calming your nervous system but sending a message to your subconscious mind that you are safe. You cannot panic when you breathe deeply. It is important to incorporate this into your daily routine, then, if you worry or notice any anxiety building, you will be able to call upon this skill in an instant and calm the nervous system down.

Do not under-estimate the benefit of deep breathing just because it seems so obvious

Deep Abdominal Breathing

The Technique:

Step 1

To start with, you may find standing is the best way to do this exercise. Ordinarily the breathing is all done through the nose, unless you have any nasal issues, in which case you can breathe through your mouth.

Place one hand on your chest and one hand on your abdomen. When you breathe using your entire lung capacity your chest hardly moves and your abdomen expands. The hand on your chest should hardly move but the one on your abdomen should move quite noticeably.

So, close your mouth and imagine that you are blowing up a balloon in your belly. As you take a slow and steady, deep breath in through your nose, your abdomen should expand because the air is going in. When you then breathe out the air goes out of your abdomen and therefore it deflates. To recap, your abdomen expands on the in breath, just like a balloon, and deflates on the outbreath. To start with breathe in for the count of 5 and out for the count of 5.

If you are struggling to connect with the deep breaths then just do a very brief strong breath into your belly so you can connect with that area and then you will be able to do the slower breaths. Do not worry if it takes you a while before you get the hang of it. Please persevere. Check out my website for a video on how to do deep breathing.

Step 2

Now slow the breaths down. The aim is to breathe in for the count of seven and out for the count of eleven. Repeat those slow and deep breaths as they will calm your nervous system down.

How to use the deep breathing

Here are a few options for using this deep breathing but ensure you do some deep breathing every day.

1. Spend five minutes focusing on your deep breathing at a slow and steady pace.
2. After you complete a task, do two slow and deep breaths. For example, when you make a drink do two of these breaths, when you go to the toilet do two of these breaths and so on.
3. When you are stuck in traffic, in a queue or sat waiting for an appointment do some deep breathing.
4. When you worry or feel anxious take deep breaths. When you make deep breathing part of your daily practice, doing so in times or worry or anxiety will be more natural for you.

Split Breathing

Another breathing option to relax and calm you is split breathing. To do this:

1. Breathe in through your nose filling up your abdomen for the count of four (slowly counting).
2. Breathe out through your mouth for the count of two (slowly counting).

Repeat this process for anything from one minute to ten minutes.

What's Your Excuse?

You breathe anyway, I'm not asking you to do anything you don't do already and it won't take up any more of your time. You have nothing to lose except anxiety and tension.

MANTRAS

As you connect with deep breaths, repeat either of these mantras or create your own personalised mantra related to breathing.

"My breath is my connection to life."

"I breathe in life."

"I breathe in calm, I breathe out stress."

28. Inner Voice Characters

A simple exercise is to put an identity to the negative inner voice. Let's start with the worry voice, which may say: *"What if I say something stupid when I am out tonight?"*

1. Consider what the 'worry voice' may look like. Give it a visual identity such as a clown, an animal, a person, a comedy character; anything you wish.
2. Then consider what the name of this 'worry voice' would be.
3. Finally, what does it sound like? Is it a wobbly voice, a soft voice, a squeaky voice? It may just sound like your normal voice.

So now you have a visual identity, a name and you recognise the sound of the voice.

For my example I have Thomas the Tortoise, who has a wobbly voice.

Now you need a more rational and positive character, it may even remind you of someone you know, perhaps a friend, relative or colleague. Do the same process for this character.

1. Consider what the 'rational and positive voice' might look like. Give it a visual identity such as a tiger, a superhero, an actor, anything you wish.
2. Then consider what the name of this 'rational and positive voice' would be.
3. Finally, what does it sound like? Is it a strong voice, a relaxed voice, a confident voice? It may sound like a person you know who is rational, confident and positive.

For my example I have Gino the Greyhound with a solid committed voice.

Here's what you do next:

Every time the worry voice fires up, so in my case Thomas the Tortoise, with those worry thoughts, Gino the Greyhound is going to jump in with a new perspective. Here are some examples:

Thomas the Tortoise *"I don't want to go out shopping in case I have a panic attack."*

Gino the Greyhound *"You have been out shopping hundreds of times and not had a panic attack. In any case you will be back in an hour."*

Thomas the Tortoise: *"I'm useless at everything I try".*

Gino the Greyhound: *"That is just not true, you are really good at all sorts of things you don't give yourself credit for. Be more respectful to yourself. Write down a list of your skills, knowledge and achievements. I bet you will surprise yourself".*

When you start to open your mind to another perspective, a more neutral and honest perspective, you realise your inner voice has been lying to you. It's been focusing on all the negatives. It has been blowing those negatives right out of proportion and not allowing anything positive in. The truth has become blurred in the process.

Your inner voice has been completely unjust and unfair to you. It's been limiting you, it's been holding you back, it's been unkind and it's now time to balance things out.

The inner voice requires a little effort on your part and soon you will see a more balanced and honest view. You will start to recognise and question some of your negative thoughts. Then you will add the positivity and take control of your inner voice.

29. Let the Fear Flow

You may know the phrase *'feel the fear and do it anyway'*. Well I am going to introduce something a little different for you.

When you let the energy of fear, or any other negative emotion, continue to flow, rather than resist it, it disappears in an instant.

The resistance we all put up because we don't want to feel certain emotions is one of the reasons why we stay stuck in those emotions. The negative emotion then gets agitated and has nowhere to go so it hangs around; it may even become more intense.

EXERCISE – Don't Skip It!

Take six to twelve deep belly breaths – slow and deep until you feel relaxed.

Consider an event that still has an emotional charge for you. Try this with something minor to start with, perhaps something that has irritated you. Let the irritated feeling flow, open yourself up to it as if you are allowing it in. Notice when you do this it goes in an instant. If the feeling hasn't gone, then you haven't fully opened up or you are focusing on aspects of the event and not the energy of the emotion.

Allow your body language to be open and relaxed and focus on letting the energy in. You may even like to say *"irritation, I openly and lovingly invite you in"* as you breathe calmly. Imagine you are opening the door of your heart to the feeling. Be honest; letting the feeling in isn't going to hurt you so open up, breathe deeply and let it in.

Once you have successfully used this on the lesser emotions, try it on a more intense emotion.

This is one of the simplest techniques there is but there is one reason why some people struggle with it and that is because they have not truly opened up to the flow of the energy. When you let down the wall of resistance, the energy can flow and shift.

Resistance is a barrier, which keeps it locked in there. Let the energy in, allow it to flow and it will be gone in an instance. This way you open up to a much more positive and higher vibration.

MANTRAS

"Fear is just an energy, I create powerful, strong and courageous energy."

"I allow all feelings to flow through me, releasing judgement and relaxing through my breath."

"As I open up and allow this emotion to flow, I am releasing it to create beneficial energy."

30. Circle of Excellence

You may recall this from the chapter on bullying but this exercise can be used for many difference purposes.

You can do this in your imagination or physically. With this particular exercise I do prefer people to do it physically whenever possible.

Before you begin, think of a situation where you would like more confidence (or any other feeling or skill that you are seeking). For example, this may be to assert yourself more or to be more confident at social events.

This is often useful to do with a friend acting out one part – such as the part of a bully or an interviewer or someone you meet socially. They will play a role in whatever situation you choose.

Below is the format and further below are some examples. I am using confidence for this example but you may select some other feeling or skill.

1. Imagine you have a circle in front of you – big enough to stand in. This is the Circle of Excellence. You can only stand in here when feeling the positive emotion - eg confidence.
2. Recall a time when you felt confident. This may be partaking in a hobby you enjoy, singing in the shower, being with friends and family. Select absolutely any event when you felt confident.
3. Recall those confident feelings and bring those feelings into you, build yourself up with confidence, what you heard at the time and what you saw. Get into that confident energy.
4. Bring in some confident music. Select whatever music feels right for you, which gives you the feeling you are seeking.
5. Now the confidence should be building. Once you feel an increase in confidence step into the circle and act that part with confidence.
6. Keep the confidence flowing. When you feel the confidence drop or you feel you have acted the part out well, step out of the circle.

7. Consider what was good about your performance and what needs more improvement and give that some focus on the next practice.

8. Keep repeating this at least six times, aiming to improve on each occasion. Each time you practice this helps to connect your mind and body with the feeling you are seeking to achieve. You are re-programming your subconscious mind and your energy!

9. Ensure you repeat this process, ideally every other day.

The more you tap into the feelings you want to have, whether they are confidence, calm, happiness or any other feeling, the easier it will be for you to access those when you want to or need to.

The other good thing about the Circle of Excellence is that you can take it anywhere with you. In your mind you can sit in it, stand in it, lie in it and nobody else needs to know what you are doing.

The Circle of Excellence may go something like the example below. I am going to apply this exercise now to an anxiety workshop I will be running this weekend.

1. I am imagining the Circle.

2. I feel confident when I am racing my bike.

3. I feel like I am strong and powerful, I am in my own zone, I don't care what people think of me when I'm riding, I feel as if I have a shield of strength protecting me. I am confident in my ability to ride and race well. In this state, I cannot be intimidated.

4. On the bike I think of music by Queen because I've performed well in the past when listening to the group and my song is *"Don't Stop Me Now".* That song really energises me and I always feel good when I hear it.

5. I think about some of my best performances which makes me feel even more confident. Now I am stepping into the Circle of Excellence. I am going to run through my opening lines at the workshop "Good morning everyone, I'm so pleased you came here because there is lot of information that I am going to share with you."

6. I step out of the Circle.

7. I am pleased with the opening line but now want to work on what I will say next.

8. I return to the confidence that I have when riding my bike and repeat the process, aiming to improve with each time I step into the Circle.

A Circle of Excellence for bullying may go something like this (this is best done with someone playing the part of the bully):

1. I am imagining the circle.

2. I feel confident when I am racing my bike.

3. I experience the same positive feelings as listed earlier. It is important to connect with the positive feelings and energy.

4. I think of my song; *"Don't Stop Me Now"* by Queen.

5. I think about some of my best performances, which makes me feel even more confident. My friend acts out the part of the bully; *"Four eyes, you are so ugly, I'm going to smash your face in".*

   Now I am stepping into the Circle of Excellence. I respond *"It's fine by me if you think I'm ugly because I know I'm fab. Ugliness comes from the words people use and their actions, not what they look like."* Of course you may keep your response short such as *"whatever", "grow up"* or *"I'm too busy for this nonsense. Shall we start again with something more positive?"*

   If you want to throw the bully off course you may wish to ask *Are you ok? Can I help you?"*

6. I step out of the Circle.

7. I feel I could have said it with a bit more confidence and commitment but am happy with the wording so I work on creating more confidence for next time.

8. I return to the feeling of confidence I have when riding my bike and repeat the process, aiming to improve each time I step into the Circle.

Don't miss this out because you feel silly doing it. I'm not asking you to stand up in public and do this. Do it in a place you feel safe but commit to it. Remember, the young girl used this to great effect and told the bullies where to go.

31. Become Your Own Adviser

I've already highlighted the troublesome impact of over-analysing. Now it's time for you to turn that around and start to be a more helpful adviser to yourself.

1. Think of some situations when you have worried about something which turned out much better than you expected. Write these down.
2. Write down what you thought at the time of each situation.
3. Write down the reality of each situation. What was the actual outcome?
4. Then write down, if you could go back in time, what advice you would give to yourself in each of those situations.
5. Based on this, write down how you would deal with those situations now.

Here is an example:

Situation when I worried: At work, I realised I had sent out the uncorrected draft of minutes of a meeting.

What I thought: I was going to be in trouble with my boss.

Reality: I told him what I had done and he was understanding and appreciated my honesty.

If I could have given myself advice at that time it would have been: What is done is done, you rarely make mistakes and it's not the end of the world. People appreciate that mistakes happen and you can resolve it very easily. Just do what you need to in order to rectify the situation.

If the same situation occurred again: Remind myself that I rarely make mistakes and it wasn't a major disaster and could be resolved the following day very easily. If my boss did over-react then it would be his shit, I'm not allowing myself to take that on. Own up to the mistake, get it resolved and move on. No harm done.

Going forward you can use this same principle. When a situation occurs give yourself some constructive advice as if you are advising a good friend.

Summary

This helps to train your brain to focus more realistically and to act in a more problem-solving manner rather than negative and panic driven way.

Since writing this book, I have noticed that when my mind is drawn to a possible negative outcome, I easily pull myself back and recognise that chances are, that won't happen. It's all about re-training that anxiety brain.

32. Tap it Out

Emotional Freedom Technique (aka Tapping) has raised its profile over the past few years in the western world.

Tapping was derived from Thought Field Therapy (TFT). It was Dr Roger Callahan who first discovered that by tapping on meridian points on the body, people started to feel better. The meridian lines link and connect with different areas of the body. For example, tapping under the eyes links with the stomach.

It was Dr Callahan who invented TFT. TFT uses different tapping sequences depending on the triggers or emotions being addressed. In turn, each category of issue to be overcome, has a different set of algorithms. This system is therefore more complicated than Emotional Freedom Technique and it is less likely that the majority of the public would find this a usable technique without the presence and leadership of a therapist.

It was Gary Craig who simplified the process by creating a system of tapping whereby you didn't need to know which point to tap on, you just tapped through the same sequence no matter what the issue to be addressed. You do this while focusing on the issue. This has made the tapping process much easier and usable by everybody.

I am now going to break down the tapping process into segments.

The Tapping Points

First of all you should become familiar with the tapping points.

EFT Tapping Points

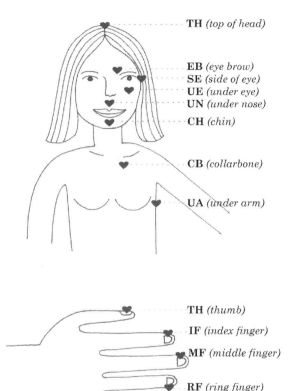

Diagram by Amy Branton. Copyright Wendy Fry.

I tap quite softly and fairly quickly. It certainly should not be painful or uncomfortable. Some of the eye points can give people a bit of a surprise until they are used to them although less likely if you are tapping on yourself. I do not tap for a set number of taps, just as long as it takes me to say each phrase.

Exercise 1 - Get used to the Tapping Points

The tapping points in sequence should be:

Karate Chop Point (side of hand)

Top of Head (nearer the back)

Eye brow (where it starts)

Side of Eye (follow eye socket)

Under Eye (follow eye socket)

Under Nose

Chin/Under Lip (where we have an indent)

Under Collarbone

Under Arm (in line with bra strap for women/nipple for men)

Side of Thumb (alongside the nail)

Side of Index finger

Side of Middle finger

Side of Ring finger

Side of Little Finger

Spend a few days just tapping through these points until you can tap without the need to refer to the book or diagram.

Exercise 2 – Score the anxiety

Before we start the tapping phrases I would like you to score the anxiety from zero (being no anxiety) to ten (being high anxiety). Score the anxiety anywhere on that scale. Don't think too hard, just go with the first number that comes to you.

Exercise 3 – Add some wording

Once the tapping points are embedded, you can then start to add some wording. Whenever possible, my preference is to say the phrases out loud.

If you have no anxiety right now, think of something that makes you feel anxious such as socialising, being on public transport etc, and then score your anxiety in relation to that.

Now for the tapping:-

We are going to start off quite simply by tapping using these words: "This anxiety".

The only difference is the karate chop wording, which goes along these lines:

"Even though I feel anxious, I choose to let it go"

We do this three times in total:

Karate Chop: "Even though I feel anxious, I choose to let it go"
Karate Chop: "Even though I feel anxious, I choose to let it go"
Karate Chop: "Even though I feel anxious, I choose to let it go"

Now on through the other points:

Top of Head: This anxiety
Eyebrow: This anxiety
Side of Eye: This anxiety
Under Eye: This anxiety
Under Nose: This anxiety
Chin/Under Lip: This anxiety
Collarbone: This anxiety
Under Arm: This anxiety

Side of thumb (alongside the nail): This anxiety
Side of index finger: This anxiety
Side of middle finger: This anxiety
Side of ring finger: This anxiety
Side of little finger: This anxiety

Once you have completed the round of tapping, take a deep breath, have a sip of water and then check in with your score. What is the intensity for the anxiety, zero to ten, now?

Hopefully it has gone down a little or altogether but do not worry if it hasn't. There is a lot more to learn.

Go through this process a few times until you feel you have this nicely embedded before we move onto the next level of tapping.

Recap

You have learned the points. You score the feeling of anxiety after each round of tapping. You are saying the relevant phrase as you tap.

Exercise 4 – Getting more specific

Let's add a little bit more information here to clear further:

What other thoughts come to mind?

Here are some examples:

"I am anxious about going out tonight"
"I am anxious because I have a test today"
"I am anxious because I am scared of crowds"

Remember to score the intensity of the anxiety zero to ten.

This is how the next round of tapping might look:

Karate Chop: "Even though I feel anxious, I choose to let it go"
Karate Chop: "Even though I feel anxious, I choose to let it go"
Karate Chop: "Even though I feel anxious, I choose to let it go"

Top of Head: Anxious about going out
Eyebrow: This anxiety
Side of Eye: I don't know who will be there
Under Eye: This anxiety
Under Nose: Anxious about going out
Chin/Under Lip: This anxiety
Collarbone: I don't know who will be there
Under Arm: This anxiety

Side of thumb: Anxious about what to wear

Side of index finger: This anxiety

Side of middle finger: I don't know who will be there

Side of ring finger: This anxiety

Side of little finger: This anxiety

Once you have completed the round of tapping, take a deep breath, have a sip of water and then check in with your score. What is the score for anxiety, zero to ten, now?

Exercise 5 – Adding in some feelings

Let's add a little bit more information here to clear further:

Where do you feel the anxiety? It may be your head, your chest, your stomach? Just make a mental note of where you feel it.

Next what does it feel like? Metaphors or colours are great for describing the energy, that is to say: the feelings.

Here are some examples:

"This blue ball of tension in my throat"

"These butterflies in my stomach"

"This red hot band across my head"

Remember to score the intensity of the anxiety, zero to ten.

This is how the next round of tapping might look:

Karate Chop: "Even though I feel anxious, I choose to let it go"

Karate Chop: "Even though I feel anxious, I choose to let it go"

Karate Chop: "Even though I feel anxious, I choose to let it go"

Top of Head: This blue ball of tension in my throat

Eyebrow: This anxiety

Side of Eye: These butterflies in my stomach

Under Eye: This anxiety

Under Nose: This red hot band across my head

Chin/Under Lip: This anxiety

Collarbone: This blue ball of tension in my throat
Under Arm: This anxiety

Side of thumb: These butterflies in my stomach
Side of index finger: This anxiety
Side of middle finger: This red hot band across my head
Side of ring finger: This anxiety
Side of little finger: This anxiety

Once you have completed the round of tapping, take a deep breath, have a sip of water and then check in with your score. What is the score for anxiety, zero to ten, now?

Exercise 6 – What has changed?

Now, what about the feelings? Have they changed in any way? The metaphors we used can really help us. Let's assume they have changed as follows:

"This red ball of tension in my throat"
"These smaller butterflies in my stomach"

(The red hot band across the head has gone so we don't need to tap on this any more.)

Karate Chop: "Even though I feel anxious, I choose to let it go"
Karate Chop: "Even though I feel anxious, I choose to let it go"
Karate Chop: "Even though I feel anxious, I choose to let it go"

Top of Head: This red ball of tension in my throat
Eyebrow: This anxiety
Side of Eye: These smaller butterflies in my stomach
Under Eye: This anxiety
Under Nose: This red ball of tension in my throat
Chin/Under Lip: This anxiety
Collarbone: These smaller butterflies in my stomach
Under Arm: This anxiety

Side of thumb: This red ball of tension in my throat
Side of index finger: This anxiety
Side of middle finger: These smaller butterflies in my stomach
Side of ring finger: This anxiety
Side of little finger: This red ball of tension in my throat

Once you have completed the round of tapping, take a deep breath, have a sip of water and then check in with your score. What is the score for anxiety, from zero to ten, now?

Again, if there are any feelings remaining, what are they now like? You may use new colours or metaphors or any other description that feels right for you.

When I work with a client, I usually keep going until we get to a zero or perhaps a one unless there is a good reason why it doesn't go low. But at this stage, any improvement is good as you become more confident at using this technique.

Exercise 7 – Putting it all together

Let's put what you have learned together for a more complete round of tapping:

Karate Chop: "Even though I feel anxious, I choose to let it go"
Karate Chop: "Even though I feel anxious, I choose to let it go"
Karate Chop: "Even though I feel anxious, I choose to let it go"

Top of Head: Anxious about going out tonight
Eyebrow: This anxiety
Side of Eye: These smaller butterflies in my stomach
Under Eye: This anxiety
Under Nose: This red ball of tension in my throat
Chin/Under Lip: Don't know who will be there
Collarbone: These smaller butterflies in my stomach
Under Arm: This anxiety

Side of thumb: This red ball of tension in my throat

Side of index finger: Anxious about what to wear

Side of middle finger: These smaller butterflies in my stomach

Side of ring finger: Anxious about going out tonight

Side of little finger: This red ball of tension in my throat

Once you have completed the round of tapping, take a deep breath, have a sip of water and then check in with your score. What is the score for anxiety zero to ten now?

Again, if there are any feelings remaining, what are they now like? What thoughts come to mind (if any)?

Progressing with Tapping

This has been a basic introduction to Tapping. The more technical work tends to be guided by a practitioner but here are a few other tips if you wish to take the tapping further.

- You can tap on any emotion such as sadness, anger grief etc. For these you would say "Even though I feel angry (or other emotion), I choose to let it go".

- The more commonly used karate chop phase ends "I deeply and completely love and accept myself". This may seem quite strange to anyone new to tapping, which is why I often start with the phase "I choose to let it go". I also believe "I choose to let it go" has a power of its own. However, if you wish, you could try the phrase "Even though I feel anxious, I deeply and completely love and accept myself".

- You may also need to expand the karate chop phrase to be more precise. For example "Even though I feel anxious, **about going out tonight**, I choose to let it go."

Why do we focus on the negative?

Tapping is very different to hypnotherapy. In hypnotherapy you tend to focus on the positive such as "I feel empowered" or "I am confident". In tapping, you mostly focus on the issue you wish to clear because you are clearing the issue through your subconscious and energy system. By focusing on the issue while tapping, you are releasing it. Look upon Tapping as a technique which releases negative emotions and attachments to events.

Secret Tapping

If I teach a client tapping, I nearly always teach them what I refer to as Secret Tapping. This is basically tapping even when in public or in company without anyone else knowing.

You can do this in two ways:

1. *Imagine* tapping on the points and saying the words inside your head. This works because tapping is an energy-based therapy and imagining or thinking carries an energy.
2. Tap only on the hand points. It just looks like you are fiddling or can be done under a desk or table and therefore you are unlikely to draw attention to yourself. Again you can say the words inside your mind while tapping on these points.

When you are doing the secret tapping you will probably want to keep the wording quite simple but it is up to you. Secret tapping is helpful when you get stressed or anxious and need a way to feel calmer in the moment without attracting attention to yourself.

Tapping in a nutshell

Here is a quick run through of Tapping:

1. Consider the emotion/issue to clear, eg anxious, stressed, sad.
2. Score the emotion zero to ten where zero is no emotion and ten is high.
3. Are there any related thoughts, eg anxious to be out in town, sad that you argued with your brother?
4. What feelings do you have and where are they? Describe those feelings ideally using metaphors and/or colours eg 'this blue ball of tension in my throat'.
5. Put it all together in a round of tapping.
6. Take a deep breath, have a sip of water and check in on your

new score, zero to ten.

7. Are there any new thoughts?

8. What feelings have changed?

9. Continue until the issue has cleared or the score is low.

10. If you hit a roadblock, use the 9 Gamut, which follows in the next chapter.

Help! I'm too anxious to think.

If you are too anxious to think about what wording to use, keep it simple. You can say a basic phrase all through the points or even just tap. Try any of the following:

"This anxiety"

"I'm safe"

"I'm ok"

"Feeling calm"

"Breathe slowly and deeply"

The positive phrases are a different approach, which I have found to be helpful when used in this type of situation.

Build up slowly

Do not rush the tapping, otherwise you might feel you haven't gained anything from it. It is far better to take your time and get used to the points and gradually do the exercises noted in this book.

33. 9 Gamut

9 Gamut is a procedure, which is supplementary to the Tapping process. It is a great procedure if you are stuck in anxious energy and for releasing emotion and trauma. If you stop making progress with the tapping or are very emotional try the 9 Gamut procedure.

Once you have this ingrained within your subconscious you will be able to call upon it at any time. Spend some time programing it into your subconscious mind by practising it.

The good news is there is only one tapping point for the 9 Gamut procedure called the Triple Warmer point, which is part of the body's meridian system, as used in acupuncture. I also call this the trauma point.

The procedure is designed to engage both the left and right hemispheres of the brain and includes eye movements. Research reports that eye movements, such as those set in the 9 Gamut procedure, help in the reprocessing of old traumatic memories.

The tapping point for the 9 Gamut is located between the bones of the ring finger and the little finger (on either hand), approximately one inch down from the knuckles. Tap this point with two fingers as you run through the 9 Gamut procedure.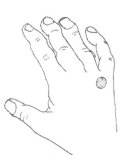

Here is the procedure:

While tapping on the Triple Warmer point:

1.   Close eyes.
2.   Open eyes.
3.   Look down to the right (keeping head in neutral position)
4.   Look down to the left (keeping head in neutral position)
5.   Roll eyes in a full circle in one direction
6.   Roll eyes in a full circle in the other direction

7.   Hum a few seconds of a song, eg *Happy Birthday to You.*

8.   Count from one to nine, rapidly but clearly.

9.   Hum a few seconds of the song again.

9 Gamut Sandwich

To use the 9 Gamut procedure within a tapping session is relatively simple. Here is how you do it:

1.   Do a round of tapping.

2.   Do the 9 Gamut procedure.

3.   Do another round of tapping.

4.   Check on your progress.

Summary

You can also use the 9 Gamut in moments of anxiety. It may be beneficial to teach someone the 9 Gamut procedure, such as a friend, partner or colleague, so they can direct you through it should you become very anxious.

We do say with the tapping, try it on everything and the same applies to the 9 Gamut procedure.

34. Control Room Dials

I make no secret of how powerful the subconscious mind can be. We can use it in many ways to address issues which get in the way of our true peace of mind and happiness.

Our emotions and feelings have energy. Anxiety has an energy. You can take charge of the anxious energy, releasing the negative and creating more positive energy.

EXERCISE – Don't Skip It!

Read through this exercise and then put it into practice. Make your first attempt a practice run.

Give yourself at least 10 minutes to do this exercise. Find a quiet and comfortable place to sit or lie. It's time to relax and get in touch with your subconscious.

Take twenty calming breaths with your eyes closed. Imagine what the inside of your mind would look like if it were a control room on a ship or flight deck.

Inside there are various dials and switches. Search for the set of dials related to emotions. You will find that there are a number of dials, which would include happy, sad, anxious, calm, peaceful, angry and no doubt many more emotions.

Search for the dial marked '*anxious*' and notice what number it is set to from zero to ten where zero is not anxious at all and ten is panic attack. I am assuming the anxious dial is turned up a few notches. Turn the dial down at least one notch. As you do, notice how your breathing slows and your body starts to relax more. You may notice your tongue rests on the bottom of your mouth, your shoulders relax downwards and your jaw loosens. Allow yourself to breathe a big sigh of relief as you turn it down.

When you feel ready, turn it down another notch. As you begin to feel yet more relaxed, you will feel your body relaxing deeper and deeper. Pleasant thoughts and calming images enter your mind. Consider what sounds make you feel calm – perhaps the sound of a waterfall, the ocean or birds singing. Each out-breath lets go of any remaining tension, each in-breath brings calm. Notice how the calming breath feels now. Take another sigh as you relax further.

You can also play with the other dials. For example, if you feel sad then turn that dial down and the happy dial up. As you do so, focus on what makes you feel happy, perhaps a television programme that makes you laugh, fun times that you have had, think of anything that makes you happy such as animals, walking on the beach, sunny holidays, soaking in a spa or going for a swim. See how far you can get the happy dial up. Recall a time when you were laughing uncontrollably, perhaps you remember tears of laughter running down your face. Connect with an image of what makes you happy. What you would hear at that time and how you would feel in utter happiness? Use as many senses as possible to connect with happiness.

Whatever it is you wish to feel more of, then focus on that as you turn up those dials in the control room. Your subconscious knows what these different emotions are and has the ability to connect with memories or fantasies, which will provide those good feelings.

If someone asked me to be in my perfect place, it would be a place full of happy animals, where they can roam around freely and I can hug and cuddle them and spend my days looking after them. I imagine flowers and lovely colourful plants and trees and places for the animals to run and play. Have I ever been in such a place? No I haven't, but I have a good idea of what would make me happy. By connecting with an image of what I would see, how it would feel to be with those lovely animals in nature and what I would hear makes me feel fabulous.

The more often you do this, the easier it becomes. It really does not matter how you connect to what you desire, you have the ability to connect with more positivity and turn down the negativity.

Summary

This could be considered a mindful exercise. You can do this at any time. It puts you in tune with your mind, body and emotions and is a great tool for making inner adjustments.

35. It's Just Energy

Every thought, every emotion, every action, every word spoken, every feeling, in fact everything has energy and we can choose to produce more positive energy or we can choose to stay in the negative. We have a choice.

Here is a simple introduction to Energy in Motion (EMO), which is an energy therapy created by Silvia Hartmann. With EMO, you do not get caught up with thoughts or events. Instead you recognise emotional pain or feeling as an *energy*, which is causing some kind of disturbance. By using this simple technique you bring your energy field back to its natural state of flow and dispense of negativity.

EXERCISE – Don't Skip It!

This exercise is best done standing up with your eyes open. If you cannot stand, then just take whatever position is best for you. The temptation is often to close your eyes but do keep them open.

1. If you currently have a feeling of anxiety, focus on that. Focus only on the feeling, not the thoughts.
2. Notice where the feeling is situated in your body.
3. This feeling is just energy. Tell yourself *"it's just energy"*.
4. Now with your eyes open take a breath in and imagine softening the energy. Remember, energy can change and transform. That is what we are doing here. As you breathe in imagine *softening* the energy. Say to yourself "*soften*".
5. As you breathe out let the energy *flow*. To allow something to flow suggests it can move and change form. Let it flow. Say to yourself "*flow*".
6. Continue this simple exercise, breathe in to soften the energy, breathe out to let it flow. *Soften and flow*. Spend a minute or two doing this.
7. As you progress with this exercise something changes. What has changed? Has the energy moved to another part of your body? Has it changed form in some way, perhaps smaller or fainter? Has it disappeared completely?

8. If there is still some energy, even if it has changed or has moved to another body part, keep repeating *soften and flow*. Breathe in to *soften* the energy, breathe out to let it *flow*.

Eventually the energy will disappear.

Here are a few things you can do to aid the process if you get a little stuck at times:

- Move position – take some steps or walk around the room and finish in a different place. Start with *soften and flow* again.
- Take a drink of water to help the body process what is happening.
- Shake your body, hands, legs, feet especially if the energy is stuck anywhere.
- If the energy is stuck in one place such as a leg, place your hand on the leg as if taking the energy and then shake your hand out.
- Try lying down to see if it creates a shift in the energy.
- Ask yourself *"what will it take to release this energy"* and listen to your intuition. You know best. Continue until the energy disappears.

If you had focused on something such as feeling anxious in a social situation, then check in with how you feel when you imagine yourself being at such an occasion. It may be the energy has completely cleared or maybe there is some more energy to clear, in which case, just run through the process again.

Summary

EMO is a great way of releasing negativity without going into thoughts and events, by focussing on the energy and using the breath to release it.

Sometimes when we have a release of emotion or energy it comes out in different ways, such as yawning or burping, so don't be surprised at how issues are released.

36. Applying the Chill Button

This particular exercise was a favourite one of a client who suffered with anxiety. The positive emotion we focused on for him was going to the gym and two specific exercises he did in his gym session. We focused on how he felt doing those exercises. This was his 'go to' when he felt anxious and it worked very well for him. It was a way to snap him out of the anxious energy and into a familiar, more positive, feeling.

EXERCISE – Don't Skip it!

1. Sitting or standing, remember or imagine a really pleasant experience, a time when you felt really relaxed and happy. This was a time when you were experiencing a very positive emotion. If you are unable to remember a positive experience, imagine what it would be like to experience something really good (just like my animal daydream earlier).

    Remember or imagine what it was like when you were experiencing the positive feeling and give the feeling a colour.

    Let the positive emotion fill your body as you imagine that colour, filling your entire body from the top of your head.... into your neck....your shoulders....into your arms.....to your hands, right to the end of your finger tips.....into your chest... your abdomen....your hips.....legs......and feet, to the tips of your toes. Totally immerse yourself in this positive feeling.

    Now, add some optimistic thoughts to these positive feelings as you think about this event and what was so good about this event. Think about what was so great about the way you felt at that time. Use as many senses as possible to recall this event.

    See the event as clearly as you can and totally immerse yourself in this experience.

    As these positive feelings fill your whole body imagine you have a button on the inside of your thumb (or anywhere else you choose). This is your chill button. Now press that button down, as you recall the positive colour, which fills your body with positive emotion. Continue to deepen those feelings and as you do, press the button down. Continue to immerse yourself in those wonderful feelings. Take a couple of minutes to do this.

2. Next think of something that would make you feel anxious. The moment you have a negative thought or feel any negative feelings press your chill button, recall your positive memory, recall your positive colour and fill your whole body with the positive emotion.

Repeat steps 1 and 2 at least three times, finish on step 1 and then move onto step 3.

3. Think of something you feel anxious about, may be an upcoming event. The moment you have a negative thought or feel any negative feelings press your chill button down, recall your positive colour and fill your whole body with that positive emotion. This time bringing those positive thoughts and feelings into *this* event, notice how calm and positive you are in *this* event, perhaps you notice a change in your breathing or posture. Imagine the event going well because you are filled with great thoughts and feelings. Keep pressing your chill button and each time you do it brings in more positive thoughts and feelings.

Continue repeating steps 1 and 3.

You can continue to repeat this process as many times as you wish. The more you repeat it, the easier it will be for you to think those positive thoughts and feel the positive emotion. In future if you were to feel any anxiety or have any of those old unhelpful negative thoughts or feelings, press the chill button down and return to your positive memory. Recall your positive colour and fill your mind and body with that positivity.

As you continue with this process you will find it so much easier to disregard those old negative unhelpful thoughts that you used to create by replacing them with positive thoughts about yourself, positive thoughts about life, positive thoughts about what could happen.

After all you have shown you have a great imagination because you have created negative scenarios and 'what ifs' for years, even though those events most probably never happened, so you can use your wonderful imagination to think of all the positive things that could happen.

Summary

The chill button can be used at any moment that anxiety starts to build or as a way of preparing for an event.

Note: If you prefer to place your chill button somewhere else, such as on your thigh feel free to do so but just ensure the button is in the same place each time so you are making a subconscious connection between the button and the good feelings. This is called an 'anchor'.

37. Talk The Talk!

If we want to change our way of thinking and behaving then we need to give our subconscious direction. Our subconscious is very obliging and willing to work with us.

Let's start with the word *"sorry"*. If you are someone who is constantly apologising you need to STOP IT. One lady came to see me and she was apologising from the moment she came into the room. She was sorry for being there, in fact, she seemed sorry for just being.

Listen to what you say and how you talk, if you are saying "sorry" for everything and being constantly apologetic, STOP IT. "Sorry" is not a word you should need to say often. Start to be aware if you are saying it out of context. If you are apologising for yourself constantly then what energy do you expect that is sending out to the world? It is saying, "I am not good enough, I do not deserve, you are better than me, everything is my fault".

No, no, and no! You must not be sorry for all and sundry, just sometimes sorry for the rare things which may actually need a proper apology.

There are many ways of working towards the life you want, and talking in a positive way is one of them. The error most people make is they focus on what they don't want. Focusing on what you don't want keeps the mind honed in on just that.

"I don't want to be anxious" said the anxious person.

"I don't want to live in fear" said the fearful person.

"I don't want to be alone" said the person who struggled to make relationships work.

We must focus on what we DO WANT in life to create the subconscious blueprint and change the energy. Say everything as if it is all possible!!

"I can have a peaceful and positive mind."

"I can be calm."

"I can be in a fulfilling relationship."

When we take things a step further we create an even more positive mind-set and energy. Talking as if we already have what it is we want would go something like this:

"I have a peaceful and positive mind."

"I am calm."

"I am united to and supported by all the people in my life."

Say it like you DO believe it. Fake it until you make it.

"I AM confident."

"I FEEL good."

"I BELIEVE in me."

What positive talk can you create? Be imaginative with it. Be outrageous even!

We need to talk the talk and then we need to walk the walk. We do this by using the mind. Our friend, the subconscious mind, is just waiting for us to put something positive in there and work with it. Give your subconscious the roadmap of where you want to be in life.

EXERCISE – Don't Skip It!

Because this is an anxiety-related book, I am going to be presumptuous and assume that it is your mission not to be anxious.

Now I want you to focus on what you DO want. I'm assuming that you want a peaceful and positive mind. When you talk in terms of *'I have"* or *"I am"* you are creating a much more positive energy. You will be sending messages to your subconscious that drive it towards what you want to achieve.

The phrase you should practise is:

"My mind is peaceful and positive."

Now take five deep breaths, close your eyes and repeat that phrase slowly and calmly 30 times. Once you have completed this, open your eyes and notice how good you feel.

Then create a phrase of your own. Take five deep breaths, close your eyes and repeat your chosen phrase slowly and calmly 30 times. Once you have completed this, open your eyes and notice how good you feel.

Going forward, it is important that you continue in this way. Whenever you notice yourself having a negative thought, about something you don't want to feel or be, STOP IT, take a breath then think about what you DO want.

38. Visualise

One of the most powerful techniques you have in your armoury is the skill of visualisation.

When you experience traumas, both 'big T traumas' and 'little t traumas' these memories stay with you. They rest not just in your subconscious mind but in the cells of your body and in your energy matrix.

A trauma can be anything, from being in a crash, being attacked, being bullied to falling over, being embarrassed or shouted at. In terms of the subconscious and our belief system, a trauma could be considered any event with a negative emotional charge.

When we experience any type of trauma, serious or minor, we store these events as little movies which are re-run in our subconscious as if they are on a loop constantly being re-played.

Those past traumas are important, no matter how insignificant or silly they appear to you now. You may believe you have 'resolved' these traumas by just 'getting through them'. Perhaps you've used medication or talked about these incidents in a bid to overcome them. However, it is most likely they are still stuck within your subconscious and still in your energy field and therefore still influencing you.

One of the things I love the most about the subconscious mind is that it does not differentiate between a real event and an event we create. This created event could be described as a daydream or visualisation. This is fabulous news as we can use it to our advantage! Sports competitors have been visualising for decades because it works. I used the skill of visualisation for my sport. I imagined myself outsprinting my opponents or being strong at the top of a climb.

Take a moment now to imagine a lemon. Notice the strong yellow colour and see the shape of the lemon. Take a moment to do this. Now imagine you take a knife and you cut the lemon open, notice how juicy it is. It is a really juicy lemon. Now take a lemon squeezer and imagine squeezing the lemon juice into a glass. Squeeze as much of the lemon juice as you possibly can into a glass. Make sure you have all of the lemon juice in the glass. Now pick up the glass and take a drink of the lemon juice.

What did you notice? Did you notice the bitter sharp taste and salivate? Most likely you will have. This shows you that just by imagining an event, your mind reacts as if it is reality and sends a message to your body to do the necessary. Anxiety causes people to imagine lots of negative scenarios, hence the response is the fight or flight symptoms even when there is no real threat. By imagining what you do want to happen the response of both mind and body can be so much more positive.

I expect David Beckham would have visualised taking free kicks or Dame Kelly Holmes imagined winning gold at the 2004 Olympics. When you show the mind what it can do, it has a blueprint to follow. This is why I tell people to focus on what you DO WANT.

By showing the subconscious mind what you could be capable of and repeating the process, it believes it, because it thinks you've already done it. Therefore, when you actually come to doing it, the subconscious mind thinks *"oh this is fine, I've done this 30 times already"*. It doesn't question it; it goes with it. You have effectively created a positive blueprint or memory.

Practice Makes Perfect

Look upon visualisation as practising for a play. When you act in a play, you would spend months rehearsing your part so that in the actual production, you would be secure and confident in your performance. Remember, that when practising you may fine-tune the smaller details. Like anything else, the more that you practise, the better you get.

Some people are naturally visual people and others are not but we can all visualise in our own way. I am not a great visualiser myself. However, by connecting to the experiences I want to achieve in the best way I can, I am much more likely to be successful than if I do not bother. And the same goes for you.

You can use other senses along with visualisation. It may be, for you, that these other senses are more relevant to how well you can imagine a future event going – such as smell, touch, taste and sound. You may already know which sense is favoured by you. Have you noticed the language you use? Here are a few examples:

Visual (sight priority) people would say:

"I see what you mean."
"I see it all clearly now."

Auditory (hearing priority) people would say:

"I hear what you say."
"That sounds good to me."

Gustatory (taste priority) people would say:

"I can taste the success."
"That leaves a sour taste in my mouth."

Olfactory (smell priority) people would say:

"The sweet smell of success."
"Something doesn't smell right about this."

Somatosensory or Kinaesthetic (touch priority) people would say:

"I can touch the success."
"Something feels wrong about this."

The most common preferences are visual and auditory, though we can often be a mix, favouring more than one sense.

I talk here mostly in terms of visualising but feel free to add any of the other senses. The more you connect with success the better.

The skill of visualisation

For some people when they visualise, it is as if they are right in the middle of the event but for others it can be more vague – go with whatever suits you best.

Spend a few moments thinking about something very familiar to you such as your bedroom (a room you are not currently in).

Where is the door and what colour is it?

Where are the windows?

Where is the bed?

What colours are the walls?

What decorations – for example, what paintings and ornaments are there?

What about the flooring – is it wood, laminate, carpet or something else entirely?

I expect it would be very easy for you to tell me about your bedroom or something you are passionate about such as your car or bicycle. This shows that you do have visualisation skills.

It really doesn't matter how clearly you see these objects because you are making a connection with your subconscious mind. All of this information is stored there.

Now we will start to make it more relevant to the issues you wish to resolve.

EXERCISE – Don't Skip It!

Think of an event that you would like to go well. It may be a social event, an interview, going to the shops or any other occasion that comes to mind.

Now spend some time imagining that event going well. Call upon as many senses as possible:

Notice what you see – no matter how vague. Just by connecting with the event and how you want it to go, you are driving your energy and your subconscious towards it; this is what creates change. Here are some possible things you will notice:

• Your face smiling

- Other people enjoying your company
- People being friendly

Notice what you hear with that success. Perhaps you will hear:

- Positive inner voice
- Your voice is relaxed and calm
- Fun and laughter

Be aware of what you feel:

- Calm
- Happy
- A sense of achievement

You may also wish to associate smell and taste with this event if appropriate. The more that you connect with this event, such as imagining it going well and having the feelings you wish to have, the more likely you will be able to reproduce this when the event happens.

Do this exercise at least another four times now and practise it daily. Bring in all the skills and attributes you need. If you need to be assertive then be assertive in your visualisation exercise. It's your imagination, there are no barriers to success here, you can be anything you want to be. You are training your mind to be successful at whatever you choose to focus on. This is true personal power.

As you progress and gain success in this area you can have another focus or element for your visualisation. Let's assume you began with assertiveness, the next event you may wish to visualise going well is a social event or a talk.

Your mind is your secret weapon. Up until recently, you didn't take charge of what it focused on but now you realise your mind is much more under your control than you ever gave yourself credit for, so use your incredible mind. Take charge of it and use it in the most powerful way.

"You can use your mind in the most negative way or the most positive way. One that will make you miserable, vulnerable, dissatisfied with life and feel out of control, the other that will help you to embrace life, reach your potential, enjoy your experiences, be brave and take charge of your future. Which do you choose?"

I have always seen myself as a 'Facilitator of Change' but not the healer or curer of all. I guide people, I help them understand different perspectives, I help them connect with the skills, knowledge and attributes that were always available to them, even if they didn't know it. However, I do not fix, cure or heal – you do that. In writing this book, I am facilitating your change but you are taking charge and doing all the fixing, curing and healing yourself. The more you commit the more success will become available to you.

Consider all the successful entrepreneurs, sports people, teachers and pioneers in this world. They achieved their success through commitment, belief, dedication and focus. The formula to success is quite basic and available to everyone, the only thing that could stop you is you. Allow yourself to access that success formula. You have everything you need to be successful in this process and success will be so sweet because YOU DID IT.

When we want something in our life to change, it is up to us to take charge of the process and create our change. Yes we should seek the help of those who 'know how' to achieve that success but never should we pass over the responsibility to them!

Empower yourself and take responsibility for your life. Create the life you want.

39. Mindful Meditation

We do not need to be experts at mindfulness or meditation in order to benefit from them. The more we practise the better we will become at them. Just like everything else we do.

Let's start at the beginning.

What is Mindfulness?

Mindfulness means being in the moment. Anxious people tend to worry about the future, often based on past experience. When we are 'in the present moment' we realise all is fine. In a mindful state, we can tune into our feelings, emotions and bodily sensations. We are more able to let the thoughts go or release the emotion on them in this state.

> *"The present moment is the only time*
> *over which we have dominion."*
>
> *Thích Nhất Hạnh*

What is Meditation?

Meditation is a state of thoughtless awareness. In an effective meditative state, there is profound and deep peace. The aim is to achieve a mentally clear and emotionally calm state. Many people report that they find this challenging but, given practice, we can get closer to this state so please be patient.

As the Dalai Lama said *"If you can't spare 10 minutes to meditate you need to spend an hour meditating."*

Whether or not you find mindfulness or meditation easy, you will benefit from practising the following exercises. Be patient with yourself and the process – do not strive for perfection. It is more important for you to make an attempt with no pressure or expectation of how it will go.

There are many resources available for both mindfulness and meditation and, like most things, it will be a case of finding what works for you and suits you best.

I am going to begin by giving you some basic exercises.

EXERCISE – One Minute Focus

We can all find a minute in the day to do a little focused exercise. This is a great one if your mind is beginning to run away.

Pick up an object, any object, it could be a mug, a pen or a bottle of shampoo. Spend one minute looking at the object, notice any words, the shape, the feel, any sounds or pictures. Observe all you can about the object in one minute. Aim for at least 5 things you will be able to recall using as many senses as possible.

When you have finished the exercise, notice what you can recall about the object.

I would be curious to know, during that exercise, how long did you spend having anxious thoughts? I imagine very little time or none at all if you were fully engrossed in the exercise.

This is a useful exercise if you start having negative thoughts or begin to feel anxious. It brings you back to *now*. This can also be a fun game of mindfulness if you do it with someone else.

EXERCISE – Thirty Breaths

Take steady deep breaths into your belly, in and out through your nose. Count each breath up to 30. If you find your mind wanders away from counting, start at the beginning again.

This exercise will relax you, give you a focus and help to balance your nervous system. Plus, you cannot panic when breathing deeply and slowly.

EXERCISE – Awareness Breath

This is another quick exercise. You breathe anyway, so this exercise is adding focus to the breath and ensuring that you focus on a full deep breath, utilising the full capacity of your lungs. Spend a minute focusing on your breath. Notice the expansion of your abdomen on the inhale and how it deflates as you exhale. Be aware of the speed of the breath. Notice any sounds you make as you breathe.

EXERCISE – Tension Release

This one is a great exercise to do when you are in a queue, waiting for someone or generally when stressed. Spend a minute being aware of yourself, how you are standing, sitting, whether you are moving, your pattern of breathing, just acknowledge any thoughts as *"there's a thought"* without any attachment to the thought. It is just a thought, nothing more.

Notice where in your body you feel warm or cool. Notice if your jaw is tense and, if so, loosen it. Is your tongue on the roof of your mouth, if so rest it on the bottom of your mouth. Are you frowning, or is there any other tension in your face, if so, relax that area. Are your shoulders up by your ears, if so drop them. Are your knees locked out (if standing), if so lightly bend them. Slow down and deepen your breathing. Do anything else that relaxes you.

EXERCISE – Create your own Magical Scene

Find a comfortable place to relax and close your eyes. Take five deep slow breaths. Imagine you have a magic wand and that you can be anywhere you want to be, doing whatever you want to be doing, with whomever you would love to be doing it with. Take some time to imagine this place as fully as possible. Connect with your senses noticing what you see, hear and feel and perhaps even taste and smell. Imagine you were there and create your own magical scene.

Come back another time and return to your scene or create a new scene or experience.

EXERCISE – C.A.L.M.

When you are stressed or anxious, try this exercise:

C – Check in with right now – you are safe.
A – Action – take five deep and slow belly breaths.

L – Look at the situation from the perspective of a neutral bystander – what advice would they give you?

M – Make new positive perspectives based on your new understanding of the situation.

EXERCISE – Calming Colour

Select some calming music and sit or lie down somewhere comfortable where you will not be interrupted. Let a colour come to mind that you feel is calming. Take five deep belly breaths – slow and deep.

Imagine sending the calming colour through every part of your body, from the top of your head to the tips of your toes. As you do this, imagine with each in-breath that you are breathing in the calming colour and with each out-breath that you are releasing any stress or negativity. Do this with your eyes closed. Allow yourself plenty of time to do this exercise, at least 10 minutes. You can always run through this more than once.

40. Coffee and Chat

Coffee has become a large part of our social culture. I would like you to take someone out for a coffee. This is a chat with someone who knows you well and talks a lot of sense. This person is confident, has good self-esteem and is someone that you respect. It is someone whose confident traits you would like to share and may be a friend, colleague or family member. Take a notepad and pen with you and make some notes.

I want you to ask your friend a few questions. You can tell them this is for an experiment or related to a book you are reading or make up whatever reason you would like but ensure that you arrange this get-together.

Write down and spend some time discussing the answers they give you to the questions below. There is no point just listening to the answer and then letting it pass you by. This will give your subconscious mind something to work on afterwards. You may even get a realisation, a light bulb moment.

Here is the list of questions for you to ask this person:

"What tips do you have for being confident and less anxious?"

I don't know what answers your friend will give you but here are some helpful tips:

"Be confident in your decisions."

"Focus on how you want to feel."

"You cannot please everybody all the time."

"Be true to yourself."

"Understand that if something did go wrong it is not the worst thing ever in the history of the world to happen."

You may wish to discuss some of these with your friend.

No doubt your friend will come up with some other answers. Explore what they have said and notice how you feel. What new perspectives are you learning and what changes can you take on board? Even if you make just one small change to begin with, that'll be useful.

The next question to ask this person is:

"What are your best personality traits?"

You have probably spent too little time thinking about your best personality traits or perhaps you have ignored them altogether because you don't feel worthy or good enough. This is a common characteristic of anxiety sufferers. If this is the case, it has to change. If you are not recognising your best traits then how can you put these to good use or attract what you desire in the world? You need to know these to create the life you want. Ensure that you write down your best personality traits.

Here are some of mine:

- I'm funny (so my husband tells me).
- I'm determined when I set my mind to something.
- I'm loyal.

Now discuss with your friend:

"What you have achieved in life."

It helps to do this with a friend because we very often ignore our achievements. Here are some of my achievements to start things off:

- I have learned to drive.
- I was three times National Hill Climb Champion for cycling.
- I run my own therapy business.

Sometimes we overlook achievements because they might seem quite ordinary or even insignificant, such as learning to drive, but that makes them no less of achievements.

Write down at least three achievements, more if possible.

And the next question to ask your friend is:

"What skills do they recognise you have?"

Again, people experiencing anxiety ignore the things they can do and focus on what they can't do. However, you are moving into a new zone and time for yourself, which appreciates your qualities, skills and attributes.

To give you an example, here are some of my skills:

- I can ski.
- I can make jewellery.
- I can hypnotise people.

Just as with achievements, you don't have to be a rocket scientist to appreciate your skills but it is important that you do. Can you cook, sew or drive? Those are all skills. Once again, write these down.

And finally….

What are any final pieces of advice your friend would suggest about your confidence, self-esteem or anxiety that would help you change and create the life that you want?

Some of these might be:

"Things always turn out much better than you expect them to which makes worrying a waste of time. Think about the best case scenario."

"Pretend to be confident and over time you will become more confident."

"Set yourself milestones, little goals, working towards a bigger goal."

"Even if that negative inner voice is trying to spoil your day, bring in your positive voice so you take the energy away from the negative."

"Expect things to go well, that way you go into them with a good energy, a positive attitude and you will find they do go well."

Whatever you have learnt from this experience, ensure you capture it and carry this forward. If you like some of the comments I have made then feel free to make a note of those. Use these skills and talents you have and if you feel there are areas for improvement, then work on those. Never look upon yourself as being flawed. We are all work-in-progress and that's a good thing.

I recall a client who came to see me to stop smoking. He was in his mid-twenties. This young man was working a full time manual job, doing extra hours at work and studying part time for a law degree. I happened to see him a year later, he had been a non-smoker for a year and had passed his degree. Amazing. This is a reminder that when we set our minds to something and persevere we can achieve incredible feats no matter what our start in life.

If anyone tells you that you cannot do something, how can they know? Their thoughts and comments are purely from their perspective, their belief system and their limitations. Are you going to be defined by someone else's perspective, belief system and limitations or are you going to give it your 100% best effort? Whatever the end result, you will know that you gave it your very best effort and I am sure you will learn along the way.

41. Flip It

For this exercise you will need:

• Two pieces of A2-size paper or bigger
• Pens (if you have lots of colours then use those)

If you don't have an A2 size piece paper, stick A4 sheets together. The reason I want something large to write on is because it makes this exercise more effective.

On the first piece of paper, write down all your worries. These may be related to work, your family or absolutely anything. Take the time to write them down filling up the piece of paper.

Now look at those worries. Recognise they are not happening because there are any number of scenarios that could happen and many of those are positive. Your brain, because it wanted to protect you, ran through many scenarios until it could find the worst possible scenario. This may sound illogical and unhelpful but it is what an anxiety brain does. In doing so it ignored the many other possible, more positive, scenarios which could happen.

Your brain took those worst case scenarios and said something like this:

"Look at this situation which I have just 'created' that 'might' happen, you can't deal with that can you, but you must deal with it, you must sort it, so think, think about it, think about it hard, really hard, you must keep thinking about it until you resolve it, you must resolve it, even though it hasn't happened and is, in reality, unlikely to happen, don't think about now, you haven't got time to think about good or fun things, think about this possible disaster really hard but you can't resolve it can you, but you must keep thinking about it, because I'm not going to let it go away, this is a real disaster, well a real fictitious disaster, a thing that 'might' happen to you, it's the biggest disaster ever and I am going to protect you by keeping it on your mind, in your mind, it's going to pop up, here and it's going to pop up there, sometimes when you don't expect it, just so you know I haven't forgotten about this thing that 'might'

happen. I'm not letting you forget about it because I want to help you, believe it or not. I know it doesn't seem like I am acting in a way that wants to help but I am trying to help. I'm here to protect you but because you haven't got a solution I am going to trigger some stress hormones for you that will put you in the fight or flight response, they won't make you feel any better at all, in fact you will feel worse, but they are there so that when this disaster, which is really a fictitious disaster, happens, you will be able to run away or fight it off even though in this day and age we tend not to run or fight because we are now domesticated creatures. I'm just here to help. So keep thinking about it because it won't go away because I won't let it. Oh and just because I'm really good to you, I'm going to set off even more of those stress hormones so you can lose sleep over this unlikely event, the thing you are worrying about, which makes you feel anxious, most if not all of the time. All this is to help you with this non-existent event, that probably won't happen."

This is what the anxiety brain has been doing to you.

What if your brain did the following when it came across the worst case scenario:

"Oh look, that's the worst case scenario but it hasn't happened and there are many other much more positive scenarios which could happen, so I'm going to focus on the positive. There is no point dragging myself down over a negative scenario I've just created in my mind, like a novel or a film, a mini-drama or pantomime that is unlikely to happen. There is no point focusing on something I have fabricated. So I'm just going to let that one go because right here and now, I'm actually ok, in fact I'm better than ok, I'm bloody brilliant. Let me check in with myself and what is happening right now. That's right, in this moment, I am fine, all is ok, I'm safe and I'm bloody brilliant. I'm going to enjoy life because if that thing which is highly unlikely to happen did happen, I'd find a way to deal with it because whatever has kept me safe up until now will continue to do so. I'm going to look at the trees and the flowers, the sea and the meadows. I'm going to enjoy things I love because there are many great and wonderful things that can happen and I am going to focus on the positives of life."

Amen to that!

Notice how different it feels to recognise the other positive possibilities. Your energy would have changed as you read the second approach. This is the reality of anxiety. It is mostly based around fiction, not fact nor truth. Even if something bad happened in the past it does not mean something bad will automatically happen in the future. It makes no sense to assume what will happen in the future based on past events because, in a court of law, past offences cannot be taken into consideration when it comes to conviction. Do you have enough evidence for this to stand up in a court of law? My guess is you do not.

And do you know what the most amazing thing is? When we do have challenging situations, we are incredibly resourceful beings and we deal with them. YOU ARE AN INCREDIBLY RESOURCEFUL PERSON. Keep reminding yourself just how resourceful and capable you are. Allow this to become one of your mantras.

"I am an incredibly resourceful person and I can deal with situations as and when they arise"

Now put a big red cross 'X' through each of those worries if they have not materialised into reality or make no sense.

In most cases, all of these worries will have an "X". I expect if there were any worries without an "X" then we are dealing with one or two actual events which are happening right NOW in your life. Otherwise if they are not happening NOW in your life they should have an 'X'. If there are any without the 'X' then it is time for you to start problem solving using all the skills, tools and resources you have available. Remember the coffee chat. Be honest with yourself and put an 'X' through those worries that are not happening now.

In reality, you have now dispensed with all or a very high percentage of worries because they either don't make sense or they are not happening now. So, rip up the paper and throw the pieces away.

Fabulous. Now we are moving onto the next phase.

Now take the other piece of paper. I want you to write positive things that can happen to you and other positive things you enjoy. This may include things that you want to achieve and the way you want to feel but write these down as if you already have these positive things. Focus the subconscious mind on what you DO want. It can include happy memories, including absolutely anything empowering and positive. This may include positive action if there were any 'real live events' you were dealing with. Here are some examples:

- I am confident
- I assert myself because my opinion is valid
- I will run 10km
- I speak up for myself
- Austria 2010 – I nailed the red ski runs
- I will learn to cook a curry
- I believe in myself absolutely and completely

Make sure that the things you want (eg confidence and to speak up for yourself) are written as if you have those things already because the subconscious mind starts to believe it and that becomes your reality. You are providing your subconscious with a blueprint or road map, guiding it with positivity of thought. Writing it, gives it more energy. Saying it, gives it even more positive energy and if you visualise it, you are almost there.

The things I want to achieve such as run 10km are in the future and has a positive focus, "I will". There is no 'try' or 'might' in there. Never say I am going to 'try' anything because 'try' indicates a lack of commitment and you most likely won't do it. When people say "I am going to *try* to get to the gym at 7am three times a week" this indicates a lack of commitment. When they say "I am *going* to get to the gym at 7am three times a week" that means they are committed. It is amazing how removing a three-letter word makes all the difference.

Including past memories such as the one I have written from Austria 2010, sets your energies into a positive frame by reminding you of good feelings and past achievements.

Now, display that paper with those positive phrases somewhere easily visible so you will see it a number of times a day. Select three that are most important and write those down on a piece of paper or card and put those in your wallet, your desk, add them to your phone or somewhere else so you can easily review throughout the day.

If you want to feel positive, you have to act positively! Every positive action you do is giving you positive energy setting your, all important, blueprint. So write it, say it, see it and act it. In time, you become it.

42. Quick Shift

I want to show you how quickly you can switch feelings. By putting this into practice, it will become a skill that you can access any time. You will also be adding to your anxiety-busting toolkit.

Please do this exercise standing if possible.

Create two distinctive areas in front of you side by side, big enough for you to stand in and move around in. The idea being that you can easily and quickly step from one area to the next.

One area is focusing on the energy you don't want, such as anxiety, sadness or any other emotion. The other area is focusing on a contrasting feeling such as courage or calm.

For this exercise let's do anxious, changing to courageous or calm. Think of something that causes you to feel anxious and something which you may do when courageous or calm. If you struggle with the courageous or calm aspect then imagine you are a courageous or calm person such as a pop star, a yoga instructor or a public speaker. This may be someone you personally know or a public figure.

Stand in the anxious area, think about what makes you feel anxious and absorb those anxious feelings. Think about your posture, what you would say or think and what feelings you have. Once those feelings have built up a little, quickly jump or step into the courageous or calm area and experience that energy, as if someone has flipped a switch. Be that courageous or calm person, talk how they would talk, stand and move how they would and feel the positive energy.

Repeat this a dozen or more times and do this exercise frequently so you can train your brain and body to switch from anxious to courageous or calm quickly and easily when you need to.

Finally

43. Therapeutic Support

One of the things I love about the good ole USA is that nearly everyone has a therapist and they talk about their therapist in the same way as they would about their dentist. They will happily say to anyone *"I'm seeing my therapist today"* or *"my therapist said..."* There is no shame in having a therapist and why should there be? Seeing a therapist can help you to overcome so many obstacles and make your life so much better.

In Britain there is still often an element of shame or embarrassment surrounding the issue of seeing a therapist. Some people feel they should be able to solve their own problems but when you have a muscle strain you go to a physiotherapist, when you have a bad back, you see a chiropractor and when you have toothache you visit a dentist. So why shouldn't you seek professional help when you have mental health or emotional problems? It makes no sense to leave these issues unaddressed and spend your life suffering.

I want my clients to feel empowered to change because I know that they **can** change and the same goes for you. Behaviours are coping mechanisms that have come into play in order to try and create a solution. As Robert Mandel said, **"every problem was once a solution to a previous problem"**. Once the trigger to an unwanted behaviour has been resolved then, in many cases, the behaviour itself subsides or disappears altogether.

The types of therapies I have mentioned here will help you to change your perspectives and resolve traumas on many levels. It is time to let go of whatever is holding you back and bring positivity back into your life.

My favoured therapies are Hypnotherapy, Matrix Reimprinting, Emotional Freedom Technique and Colour Mirrors. Resolution to problems happens on many levels, consciously, subconsciously, energetically and physically.

Ask for referrals in order to find a good therapist in your area. Sometimes it can be worth travelling to see a good therapist and, with modern technology, sessions can be conducted over the internet.

I had a client come to see me with anxiety. He wasn't sleeping, he had the shakes and couldn't concentrate at work. After three sessions with me he said he was *"back to my old self".* He told me he was pleased he felt better because the therapy had *"cost him a fortune".* It had cost him just over £300 to feel many times better than he did three weeks earlier. £300 is a very good deal for getting anyone's mental and physical health back on track. Many people spend more than that on their mobile phones and other gadgets. We pay to service our cars, why wouldn't we pay to service our most valuable assets, our mind and body?

When asked what he finds most confusing, the Dalai Lama replied:

"Man. Because he sacrifices his health in order to make money. Then he sacrifices money to recuperate his health"

The Dalai Lama

Going Forward

Get recommendations for a good therapist. Review their website and testimonials. Have a look at their credentials. Check what professional bodies they are associated with. Trust your gut instinct too.

Do not expect a magic wand. Sometimes that can happen but be fair to your therapist. You may have years of stress and trauma to work through and to expect them to 'fix' you in a session is unfair.

Good therapy is a joint process. If your therapist gives you additional things to do outside of your therapy – please do them for your benefit. Be proactive with your health and well-being. You will reap the rewards.

Insight into my therapies

I have talked a little about my favoured therapies. I have found that using these in a bespoke way works best. For each individual this is the most powerful way of achieving success.

Hypnotherapy

Becoming relaxed, or in a state of trance, enables better connection with, and access to, the subconscious mind. I have referred to the subconscious quite often in this book so let me just explain a little more about it.

Your subconscious mind is the equivalent of a vast database containing information about you and your life. It has stored inside it, every event that has ever happened to you, every conversation you have had, your likes and dislikes, behaviour learned from others, beliefs, values, habits and much more. Imagine a memory stick full of information about you and your life. This is what the subconscious is like. By accessing the subconscious through hypnotherapy, we are able to bring greater understanding to problems, find solutions and create a positive future. We process information mostly via the subconscious mind, in fact ninety five per cent of processing is subconscious and only five per cent conscious which makes hypnotherapy a fantastic tool for change.

I call the state of trance *"turning off your stress button"*. I love trance personally and judging by my clients' feedback; so do they

Emotional Freedom Technique (Tapping)

Tapping has been shown to produce powerful results. I have given you a starter's guide to Tapping. When you work with a therapist, they should be able to do the deeper work for you and you can continue to tap for yourself as you wish. Depending on how experienced you become, you could be able to work through many issues for yourself.

Matrix Reimprinting (Matrix)

Matrix Reimprinting (Matrix) is very close to being a combination of Hypnotherapy and Tapping. Developed by Karl Dawson, Matrix has become a very successful therapy. The basic use of Matrix is to tap on your 'younger self' or 'ECHO' to release a trauma. An ECHO is an energetic consciousness hologram. You are helping your 'younger self' find resolution to the trauma.

This releases the emotion and 'energy' of the event. You bring understanding about the event. You then create a new memory, which helps to let go of any negative beliefs.

Matrix can be particularly beneficial for the more challenging traumas and is best conducted under the guidance of a qualified practitioner as some issues need to be handled with extreme care.

Colour Mirrors

I do not really consider Colour Mirrors a therapy in the conventional sense. In many ways the bottles offer something unique and special. The benefits from using Colour Mirrors can happen on many levels. In reality you have to experience them to fully appreciate what they are about.

I became interested in Colour Mirrors when these amazing bottles were used on me and, as I inhaled each essence, I found the negative emotions dissipated instantly. I was also amazed at how the wording for each individual bottle was so relevant to the issues I was addressing.

This system was created by Melissie Jolly, a South African woman who I look upon as incredibly wise and spiritual. These colourful bottles are referred to as Colour Mirrors as they reflect back at us our life journey, experiences, emotions, what we are going through at the moment and many other things.

I love using the bottles as part of a therapy session or on their own either in a one-to-one session or a workshop. The Colour Mirrors are inspirational and carry so much wisdom. They help you release stress and trauma from your subconscious mind and body cells. I find that they can bring understanding, clarity and can help you change your life around. Children absolutely love them too.

Rhythmic Movement Training International (RMTi)

RMTi is also not a therapy but a way of creating positive change on many levels. It is a process, which helps to integrate primitive and postural reflexes, which have, for various reasons, either become active or never been integrated. The Fear Paralysis Reflex and the Moro Reflex are two reflexes specifically related to anxiety.

As a Consultant in RMTi, I have seen great improvements with my clients on many issues. RMTi is a movement-based approach which, over time, helps to build the brain connections needed to function well. This has to be conducted at a steady rate as building neurons is no small task. The rewards of RMTi can be invaluable.

In RMTi, the consultant assesses the client and then directs the process to make the connections within the brain. The client then continues to do the selected exercises at home and visits the consultant on a monthly basis (or as appropriate) to check on progress and decide on the next set of exercises.

RMTi can help behaviour, OCD, postural challenges, co-ordination, ADD, ADHD, dyspraxia, dyslexia, anxiety, insecurity and many other issues.

In Summary

My message is that you can change. Life can be so much better but take responsibility for your life and take action. These are my favourite therapies because they work with the subconscious and your energy system. Find a therapy or combination of therapies that work for you and see what can happen and how you can make your life so much better.

Please visit www.energyofanxiety.com to view additional information and support.

44. My Final Message

You are more powerful than you ever thought you were

You can change

You are not a victim

Those 'bad' experiences – were opportunities to learn and grow

It is your responsibility to take action

Never give up – keep moving forward

Look for the positive in every situation

You are far greater than you ever thought you were

Perfection is over-rated and steals your life

Life is a journey of experiences and lessons

Remember 'now'

Be kind to yourself

Release judgement

Guilt is a wasted emotion

You are allowed to experience joy

Laugh, laugh and laugh some more

Be amazing you

You can do it!

45. Client Testimonial

"In today's modern internet age we have all become experts in our own conditions, frantically scanning Google for suitable answers which may or may not be relevant to our particular needs! A much better place to start learning about Anxiety is to read a good book on the subject that gets us started on our road to freedom.

Ann Bowditch's book "The Energy of Anxiety" is that good book. It has been written in a clear and concise fashion and offers much more information than I thought possible. Once I started reading it I knew it was exactly what has been missing from the marketplace.

It is a book that provides real, achievable solutions rather than promising a quick fix to solve your problems by the time you finish reading it! Through the book, Ann only requires you to have the commitment to pursue your path of recovery through self- learning, together with some guided therapy solutions to free yourself from the pain and anguish of anxiety. It will help you understand how your mind works and how to challenge those unwanted feelings and emotions and help yourself to a more enjoyable life. There are plenty of simple exercises to practise to help you as you work through the Chapters, together with a section of the book solely devoted to self-help and therapy guided methods. It may be that one of these methods may not be for you and that is why this book is so good, there are plenty of different options for you to explore to find a level that you are comfortable with to help you achieve your goals.

Ann's has an incredible knowledge of many different types of therapies and how they can be used either on their own or integrated in order to achieve the desired results.

After suffering many years of mental health illness and being turned from "pillar to post" in mental health care which has become complex, I ended up getting lost in the "system". I was taking medications to mask the problems but unable to address them from a cognitive level and had hit rock bottom using disordered eating and self-harming as a coping mechanism.

I turned to Ann, whom I initially knew from cycling, for help when I thought I couldn't carry on anymore. Ann had been extending her studies and had become a highly regarded, proficient Practitioner of different but complementing techniques, and when I was struggling, I sought her help from an initial taster session that she had run.

Having worked with Ann I can honestly say that she has changed my life. It's not a quick fix option because that is not the nature of most of the manifestations that we all have and seek help for. It takes time to work through. A good analogy that I use to explain to people what Ann's different techniques have done for me, is to try and imagine that getting better is like peeling an onion. Through the sessions attended and the different type of therapies and exercises detailed in the book I have gone layer by layer of the onion to the core problems.

It was very obvious with me that the things I thought were causing me the anxieties and depression were actually just masking the real core issues. It was only by going through consistently bit by bit from each stage to the next with continuity that I made progress and am now free from the hold of self-harming and disordered eating. I live in the moment and love each one of them for what they are and what I learn from them. I am free."

Karina Jackson

Websites

The Energy of Anxiety
www.energyofanxiety.com

Ann Bowditch
Hypnotherapy & Holistic Health
www.hypnotherapy.gg

Colour Mirrors
www.colourmirrors.com

Korani
www.korani.net

Wendy Fry
www.bepositive.me.uk

EFT International
(previously AAMET)
www.EFTInternational.org

General Hypnotherapy Register
www.general-hypnotherapy-register.com

Matrix Reimprinting
www.matrixreimprinting.com

Rhythmic Movement Training International
www.rhythmicmovement.org

Ho'oponopono – About Dr Len
www.bluebottlelove.com/hew-len-hooponopono

Guild of Energists
www.goe.ac

Acknowledgements

Thank you to my husband, Mike, for always believing in me, encouraging me and supporting me in whatever I endeavour to do.

I am forever indebted to Wendy Fry who has been an absolute shining star. Your support, advice and encouragement has been invaluable. Much love to you.

To all my many great tutors. I always feel fortunate to have manifested wonderful tutors no matter what I am studying. A special mention to Korani who has gently and supportively continued to be there and is such a guiding star with beautiful energy.

Thank you to Korani, Caroline Wickham, Chelsie Blondel, Jo May, Karina Jackson, Wendy Fry, Georgie Le Cras, Deborah Wiggins-Hay, Tara Brehaut, Sonja Greenfield and Janice Graham for taking the time to read my scribblings and provide valuable feedback.

An extra special mention to Jo May, for her sound advice and being my podcast buddy.

To the Pink Dragons, my tribe, who embrace my quirkiness, are always supportive and fabulous.

A special thanks to my greatest teachers of all: my wonderful clients. Without you I would have never been able to learn so much.

Thank you to everyone that has provided me with those life lessons that have enabled me to help others.

Finally to everyone involved in helping me to get this book out there – you've been awesome.